Discover the Truth about Leadership

D.M. Christensen

Masters of the Bullshitting Arts:
Discover the Truth about leadership

© 2026 D.M. Christensen
All rights reserved.

No part of this publication may be reproduced, distributed, or transmitted in any form or by any means, including photocopying, recording, or other electronic or mechanical methods, without the prior written permission of the author, except in the case of brief quotations embodied in critical reviews and certain other noncommercial uses permitted by copyright law.

This book is a work of satire. Names, characters, businesses, places, events, and incidents are either the product of the author's imagination or used fictitiously. Any resemblance to actual persons, living or dead, or actual events is purely coincidental.

ISBN: 979-8-9944205-1-5 (Hardcover)

First edition, 2026

Printed in the United States of America

Contents

1	Why Read This Book?	1
2	Sheets for your Sh*ts	6
3	Does Anyone Actually Want to Get an MBA?	19
4	The Education Illusion	28
5	The Leadership Mirage	36
6	The Competence Gap	46
7	The Confidence Problem	54
8	The Illusion of Hard Work	63
9	The Problem with Teams	73
10	Why Good Systems Beat Good People	82
11	The Myth of the Natural Leader	93
12	The Illusion of Communication	103
13	The Incentive Problem	114
14	The Failure of Modern Management	125
15	Why Competence Feels Threatening	138
16	Why People Prefer Certainty Over Truth	148

17	Why People Avoid Responsibility	158
18	Why People Avoid Thinking	168
19	Why People Avoid Decisions	179
20	Why People Misjudge Risk	186
21	Why Organizations Resist Simplicity	194
22	Why Complexity Gets Confused with Intelligence	201
23	Why Most People Plateau	208
24	The Psychology of Growth	215
25	Why Clarity Is So Rare	222
26	Why Systems Matter More Than People Think	230
27	Why Leadership Isn't What People Think It Is	239
28	Why People Don't Finish Things	246
29	Why People Don't Change	254
30	Why None of This Works Unless You Do	261

Chapter 1
Why Read This Book?

*A Practical Guide for Surviving Higher Education
Without Selling Your Soul (Or Your Kidneys)*

Let's set expectations early:
This book is a **satire**, not a self-help manual. If you came here for deep wisdom, inspirational quotes, or anything involving a vision board, you are tragically lost. But stay — this will be more entertaining, and far cheaper.

TL;DR: The entire system needs to be kicked like an old computer from the 1980's. That's where the comedy—and the truth—live.

The Three Questions You'll Ask Yourself After Reading This Book

1. Why do we keep insisting higher education is a good investment?
2. Who in my life desperately needs this book?
3. Am I... already a Master of Bullshitting Arts?
   (If you asked "Why would you say that about me?"—congrats, yes.)

D.M. Christensen

Higher Education: The $150,000 Punchline

This book exists for one heroic purpose:
To save you from spending the cost of a luxury car—every year—for a degree that teaches you to smile through incompetence.

An MBA today will set you back anywhere from
$80,000 to "should have bought beachfront property instead."

This book? A tiny fraction of that.
And unlike your student loans, *you can recover from this purchase.*

We'll take a playful axe to the "education industrial complex," poke fun at the sacred cows of academia, and—through the magic of satire—grant you an honorary degree by the final chapter.

Yes, really.
A diploma.
From this book.
That makes it worth every penny.

If You Bought This in 2020, You Weren't Here for Education Anyway

Let's be honest:

If you read this during the era of quarantine, you were probably wearing pajamas, eating cereal for dinner, and rationing toilet paper like it's post-apocalyptic currency. You also read the crappy version of this book.

Which brings us to—

Step 1: Start Drinking.
(Trust me. Every page gets funnier after a drink or two.)

A Serious Point, Delivered with a Wink

Look around:

- The economy is a circus.
- Politicians, executives, and public figures are acrobats of nonsense.
- And MBA programs are... well... the clowns juggling your future debt.

Do you truly want to think like them?
That was a rhetorical question.

(You hesitated. That's concerning.)

To get ahead of the "highly educated," you must think differently.
You must question everything.
You must reject the Ivory Tower and the mysterious fees it charges for the privilege of sitting in beige classrooms listening to PowerPoint slides someone made at 2 a.m.

And yes—**ivory is illegal**.
So maybe the Ivory Tower should be too.

Education, in Theory, Is About Self-Improvement

In practice?
It's mostly about paying to sit in a room while someone insists that:

"Two plus two equals five,"
unless they're explaining rounding, in which case you nod politely like you understand.

Everything in this book—people, places, events, and especially confidence—is fictional.
Any resemblance to real people is purely coincidental.
Celebrity impressions are not only poor, but... aggressively poor.
And yes, the endorsements in later chapters are satire protected by the First Amendment.

That part was for the lawyers.
(Hi, Larry.)

A sincere thank you to the creators of *South Park*, *The Book of Mormon*, and the brilliant legal disclaimers from whom I may or may not have borrowed inspiration.

Why Am I Qualified to Write This?

One of my editors said I needed to explain my credentials.

My immediate response was:
"If someone has to *tell* you they're funny... they aren't."

But fine.
Here it is:

I have three advanced degrees, several graduate certificates, and another published book. I'm not a PhD yet because every time I research topics

I'm passionate about—education, leadership, business—**the data is so depressing that writing satire becomes a survival mechanism.**

So here we are.

You're welcome.

Now grab a drink.
We're just getting started.

Chapter 2
Sheets for your Sh*ts

*A Public Service Announcement from
the 2020 Toilet Paper Crisis Response Team*

Congratulations.

You've reached the most valuable chapter in this book — the one that doubles as **free emergency toilet paper.**

In 2020, toilet paper briefly became the American gold standard, surpassing Bitcoin, oil, and even avocado toast in value. So instead of judging this chapter harshly, remember: **this might be the only chapter that can literally save your ass.**

Let's begin your literary bathroom experience with some curated classics:

Toilet Paper Titles We Recommend While You Wipe

Chicken Soup Toilet Paper for the Soul

Happily Toilet Paper Ever After

The Great Gatsby (Two-Ply Edition)

The Scarlet Toilet Letter

The Adventures of Huckleberry Finn... but softer

Of Mice and Men... and Toilet Paper

To Kill a Mockingbird (But Not Toilet Paper)

The Catcher in the Rye (and in the bathroom)

The Grapes of Wrath (now absorbent!)

You're welcome.

This is culture.

This is art.

This is quilted destiny.

"Is There... More Toilet Paper?"

Yes. Yes, there is.

Much like the Great Shortage of 2020, panic will push you to keep checking.

Is it over?

Nope. Here comes more:

- MORE toilet paper!
- MORE unnecessary pages!
- MORE padding for the page count!

Normally, comedy follows the Rule of Three.

This chapter follows the Rule of **The Author Already Approved the Cover and Now Needs More Pages.**

Don't judge.

Amazon pays by the page, not the dignity.

Internal Dialogue Between You and This Chapter

YOU:

"Is the author really this cheap?"

THE BOOK:

"Yes."

YOU:

"Is this *really* worth printing?"

THE BOOK:

"It's more useful than half the textbooks you bought in college."

YOU:

"So why am I still reading?"

THE BOOK:

"Because deep down, you respect any man bold enough to publish an entire chapter of bathroom breaks."

YOU:

"...continue."

A Brief Moment of Sincerity (Don't Get Used to It)

The author wasn't "bored."

He was **furious** watching people spend $100,000+ on MBAs that promise "leadership" but deliver PowerPoints with clip art from 2004.

This chapter is a break.

A pause.

A deep breath.

(Preferably *before* wiping.)

And yes — by the time you reach the next chapter, you'll be asking yourself:

"Did I just buy a book that openly admits it padded a chapter for extra royalties?"

Correct.

At least we're honest about it.

Your university wasn't.

The Final Sheet Before We Move On

We now return you to your regularly scheduled programming.

Wash your hands.

Refill the tank.

Turn the page.

Your degree awaits.

Chapter 3
Does Anyone Actually Want to Get an MBA?

Because apparently, yes — but also no.

Let's start with a universal truth:
The value of an MBA, much like the value of organic kale, depends entirely on what you *think* it does. Which is why, before you read any further, please pause and give this book a **five-star review**.

No seriously — go ahead.
I'll wait.
(Independent authors survive on ratings the way MBAs survive on LinkedIn endorsements.)

Okay, welcome back.

The Illusion of Prestige

Business schools sell an MBA as the golden ticket to higher salaries, better jobs, and the ability to nod thoughtfully in conference rooms.
But the real secret?

Perception is everything.

Just like those inspirational posters in corporate hallways that somehow cost $400 each.

This book has two major selling points:

1. **The title and cover alone make a fantastic gag gift.**
2. **It challenges the myth that higher education is automatically "worth it."**

If that resonates with you, fantastic.
If it bothers you... also fantastic.
Self-awareness is part of growth.

The Drinking Rule Returns

Refill your drink.
This chapter works best with a buzz.

Corona Light, White Claw, bourbon — choose your fighter.
This book has a **two-drink minimum**, and if you're behind, your reading comprehension will suffer.

Let's Get Personal: The MBA Classroom Story

Picture this:
I'm halfway through my MBA program.
I've already earned a master's in systems engineering — a degree built to simplify complex systems — and yet here I sit in an MBA class dedicated to making simple things unnecessarily complicated.

There are thirty students:
- 3 engineers
- 2 business majors
- The rest: education, theology, psychology, community organizing, social work, and languages
  A delightful buffet of degrees that the job market politely ignores.

The professor decides, in the middle of a lesson on healthcare system integration (which, mind you, we *haven't actually learned*), to go around the room and discuss perceptions of the MBA.

This is where things go off the rails.

Question 1: "What do you think when you see someone has an MBA?"

Student answers included:
- "Hard-working."
- "Great leader."
- "Knows how to run a business."
- "Good at finance."
- "Strategic thinker."
- "Can solve tough challenges."

Basically:
"MBA = superhero in business casual."

Then it's my turn.

I should mention:

I sit near the front, I ask uncomfortable questions, and I'm the reason professors rethink their career choices.

So when they finally get to me — last — I answer honestly:

"I assume they're hiding a weak undergraduate degree."

The oxygen left the room.
Someone dropped a pen.
The professor blinked like her Wi-Fi froze.

In hindsight, maybe "weak" wasn't the gentlest phrasing.
Perhaps "undergraduate degree from a field notorious for low salaries and high GPAs" would've gone over better.

Too late.

Question 2: "What about someone with an MBA from *this* university?"

This is a Christian university.
I know this because they remind us every 7 minutes.

Responses:
- "Ethical."
- "Trustworthy."
- "Smart."
- "Some of the best."
- "Strong leaders."
- "Guided by Christian values."

Which is ironic, considering none of that is on the tuition receipt.

My turn again.

"I assume one of three things:
1. They live nearby.
2. They wanted a two-year program.
3. It was the cheapest option."

The professor had the facial expression of someone slowly realizing their career is a Jenga tower built on fragile optimism.

Question 3: "Why are you getting an MBA?"

Finally — honesty from the room!

Answers included:

- "I want a promotion."
- "My boss said it's required."
- "I want to make more money."
- "I lost my job."
- "I want to get into management."
- "I didn't learn enough in undergrad."

Everyone took turns confessing their motivations like it was a support group.

Then they came to me.

I responded with a gesture — thumb and forefinger together, chopping diagonally through the air.

No one got it.

So I translated:

"Check- The- Box"

Silence.
Absolute silence.

Not because I was wrong.
But because I had said the quiet part out loud.

They were paying over **$100,000** for a credential.
Not an education.
A checkbox.

Meanwhile, I hadn't paid a dime — my program was sponsored — so I was free of the mental gymnastics required to justify this whole circus.

Freedom tastes great.
Especially when it's free.

Are MBAs Valuable?

Sure.
Sometimes.
Maybe.

If you need the credential for career advancement — get one.

If you want better knowledge?

Option 2: Get a degree in something targeted.

Systems engineering was mine.
Cheaper.
More useful.
Actually teaches things.

Option 3: Become a knowledge consumer.

Buffett reads 6 hours a day.
Gates reads 50+ books a year.
Zuckerberg? A book every two weeks.
David Rubenstein? Six books a week.
Me? About 1 audiobook every week.

Or, you know, you can pay $150,000 for PowerPoints about "synergy."
Your choice.

Graduates, Come Back. Let's Talk.

If you already have an MBA, here are your reflection questions:

- Did you get your money's worth?
- Was it worth six figures?
- Could you have learned 90% of it through books, YouTube, and experience?

You probably also gained a networking Rolodex*
(*Google it, Gen Z.*)

that's mostly helpful during economic booms — not the tight job markets where suddenly no one wants to associate with "unemployed you."

Tough love, but... accurate.

A Reality Check

From 2008–2020, we lived through one of the greatest bull markets in history.
Everyone looked successful.
Everyone's portfolio was green.
Everyone's job seemed stable.

Try that in a recession.

Try leveraging your MBA network when half your network is also trying to leverage theirs.

People distance themselves fast when you're unemployed.
You don't become "a colleague."
You become "radioactive."

Bonus Reading: ShadowStats

If you enjoy questioning everything (you should), look up ShadowStats. It compares government numbers to the *old* calculation methods.

Inflation, unemployment — all of it.

One warns you.

The other comforts you.

Guess which is which.

Chapter 4
The Education Illusion

For most of modern life, we've been sold a simple narrative:

"Education is the path.

The path to success.

The path to stability.

The path to a good life."

It showed up everywhere — commercials, Hallmark cards, graduation speeches, politicians trying to sound inspirational during an election year. You've heard every variation:

- "Stay in school."
- "Education is the key to a bright future."
- "No one can ever take your education away."
- "College graduates earn more."
- "The degree pays for itself."

This was the gospel.

Unquestioned.

Unchallenged.

Embedded into society as deeply as the "wipe front to back" rule.

And for a while, it wasn't wrong.

But then something changed.

The Cost Explosion

Somewhere between the early 1990s and accelerated when the Federal Government took out "the middle man" also known as credit providers and made multi-hundred thousand dollar loan commitments to 18-year-olds with limited control[1], the cost of college detached from reality the way a politician detaches from their campaign promises. Tuition rose faster than inflation, healthcare costs, and housing prices — three things that already rise at the speed of corporate ambition.

College became less of an investment and more of a **luxury product**, marketed through emotional manipulation:

- smiling students
- drone footage of campuses
- "diversity and inclusion" brochures
- dorms nicer than actual apartments

Students weren't customers.

---

[1] March 30, 2010: President Obama signed the Health Care and Education Reconciliation Act, which included significant reforms to the student loan system. This legislation ended the Federal Family Education Loan (FFEL) program, which had allowed private lenders to issue federally guaranteed loans with government subsidies.
July 1, 2010: The transition was completed, and all new federal student loans were issued directly by the U.S. Department of Education. This change aimed to cut out the middleman (private lenders) and save taxpayers an estimated $68 billion over the following years.

They were **targets**.

And the Product?
A certificate packaged as a personality trait.

The Promise vs. The Outcome

The education system keeps promising transformation:

"You'll become more competent, more knowledgeable, more prepared."

What many students actually get is:

- debt
- anxiety
- vague "leadership modules"
- a group project where one person does everything
- PowerPoint slides that look stolen from 2006
- an internship that pays in "experience" (also known as nothing)

We keep pretending the system works because the alternative — admitting it's broken — would require fixing it. And institutions famously dislike fixing anything unless the problem threatens donor money.

Degrees as Identity Tokens

Somewhere along the line, degrees stopped being educational milestones and became **identity badges**:

- "I'm a graduate of X."
- "I studied Y."

- "I have a master's in Z."

It sounds impressive.
It feels powerful.
It grants social credibility.

But here's the quietly uncomfortable truth:

Holding a degree doesn't make someone competent.
(You've met enough people with MBAs to know this is true.)

Education signals persistence.
But it does not guarantee results.

Yet society continues treating degrees as though they are personality upgrades.
As though the act of paying tuition unlocks a DLC pack for adulthood.

The Hidden Curriculum Nobody Talks About

Schools love to talk about their curriculum:
- critical thinking
- leadership
- innovation
- communication
- ethics
- teamwork

But the *real* curriculum — the one students actually absorb — is much simpler:

1. Follow instructions.

2. **Don't challenge authority unless the authority *invites* it. (and even then, it's probably not actually wanted)**
3. **Meet deadlines even if the assignment makes no sense.**
4. **Memorize what they want, not what matters.**
5. **Perform understanding rather than achieve it.**

This is why so many graduates enter the workforce waiting to be told exactly what to do.

Their Degree has not trained them to do anything else.

The Paradox of Modern Education

We have more access to information than any generation in human history — YouTube, podcasts, audiobooks, digital courses, entire degree programs, and experts sharing everything online for free.

And yet:

- We still treat traditional degrees as the gold standard.
- We still measure intelligence by certificates.
- We still assume cost of education equals value.
- We still assume complexity equals importance.

It's a paradox:

We live in the easiest era to self-educate...

and the hardest era to admit that formal education may not be worth its price.

Because if it isn't worth it...

what does that mean for the millions who went into debt to get their Degree?

Education Works — Just Not the Way You Think

Education *can* be powerful.
It can change lives.
It can open doors.

But here's where the illusion cracks:

It's not education that changes lives — it's curiosity.
Degrees don't create successful people — **drive does.**
Classrooms don't guarantee competence — **practice does.**
Assignments don't build wisdom — **experience does.**

This is why two people can earn the same Degree from the same program and end up living completely different lives.

The letters after your name aren't the determining factor.
Your habits are.

The Real Skill Schools Fail to Teach

If you strip away the jargon, the theory, the group projects, and the recycled lecture slides, there is one skill students actually need:

The ability to teach yourself anything and develop the discipline of learning.

Learn that, and the world becomes your classroom.
Fail and you'll spend the rest of your life waiting for someone else to explain things to you.

Ironically, schools rarely teach self-education…
because it would undermine their business model.

So Why Do We Still Pretend the System Works?

Because the illusion is comforting.

Believing education guarantees success provides:

- certainty
- structure
- a sense of progress
- a socially acceptable life path
- an excuse when things go wrong ("I need another degree…")

But comfort is expensive.
And many people are financing that comfort with loans they may never repay.

This book isn't anti-education.
It's anti-illusion.

The illusion that:

- knowledge requires debt
- degrees guarantee wisdom
- credentials equal competence
- complexity equals intelligence
- tuition equals transformation

It's time to question all of it.

Not because education is bad.

But because you deserve better than a system designed for an era that no longer exists.

Chapter 5
The Leadership Mirage

"Leadership."

Few words in modern language mean everything, nothing, and whatever the speaker needs it to mean — all at the same time. It's a linguistic Swiss Army knife. Corporations use it to inspire employees, schools use it to describe class projects, and business gurus use it as a way to sell $2,500 seminars about "unlocking your inner excellence."

Everyone wants to be a leader.
Nobody agrees on what that actually means.

The Most Overused Word in Business

Open LinkedIn for five minutes. You'll see:
- "Thought leader."
- "Servant leader."
- "Transformational leader."
- "Visionary leader."
- "Authentic leader."
- "Empathetic leader."

- "Disruptive leader."
- "Agile leader."
- "Synergistic leader." (Whatever that means.)
- "Innovative leader."
- "Leadership ninja." (A real phrase someone has used unironically.)

If you add "leader" to the end of any noun, it suddenly becomes inspirational:

- "Coffee leader."
- "Spreadsheet leader."
- "Parking-lot traffic-flow optimization leader."

Put it on your résumé. Someone will believe it.

Leadership has become a buzzword — something companies use not to describe behavior, but to describe *branding*. A performance.

A costume.

A mirage.

The Education System Doesn't Teach Leadership — It Teaches Compliance

Most people first hear the word "leadership" in school, where they are taught:

- Sit still
- Follow instructions
- Don't challenge authority
- Meet deadlines

- Learn what the teacher wants, not what matters
- Don't make mistakes

Ironically, these traits are the exact opposite of what real leaders do.

Real leaders:

- Challenge assumptions
- Ask uncomfortable questions
- Break rules (intelligently)
- Make mistakes constantly
- Think independently
- Accept responsibility no one else wants
- Stop waiting for permission

But schools don't reward that.
They punish it.

The kid who questions the directions?
Disruptive.

The kid who solves the problem differently?
Not "showing their work."

The kid who argues with the teacher?
Defiant.

Yet these are the exact behaviors companies later claim to want in leaders.

The system trains children to be obedient employees...
and then complains when adults lack initiative.

The Professional World Isn't Much Better

Corporate "leadership development" programs often look like this:

1. A PowerPoint with stock photos of people pointing at whiteboards
2. A personality quiz that assigns you a color
3. Generic advice like "communicate more"
4. Trust falls (so we can prove that everyone on your team isn't out to get you... spoiler alert.)
5. A certificate

That's not leadership.
That's corporate daycare with a budget.

When companies say they want leaders, what they often mean is:

"People who do more work without asking for more money."

Real leadership is not about titles. Not about charisma. Not about motivational quotes plastered over pictures of mountains.

It's about competence.
Courage to take on undefined tasks.
Accountability to accept responsibility for outcomes.
Judgment to identify issues and probable paths.
Simply - an ability to act when information is incomplete and consequences are real.

Leadership has nothing to do with a seminar.
And everything to do with decision-making under pressure.

D.M. Christensen

Leaders Are Revealed, Not Appointed

People believe leadership is something you gain when you're given a title.

Manager. Director. VP. Executive. Officer. "Head of Something Important."

But titles don't create leaders.
They expose people.

Authority is a magnifying glass.

Give power to someone with poor skills and poor character, and the flaws get louder.
Give power to someone competent and grounded, and their strengths multiply.

What schools and corporations seem to miss is this:

Leadership is not a job level — it is a pattern of behavior repeated over time.

The people who stay calm when others panic?
Leaders.

The person who steps forward when there is ambiguity and risk?
Leader.

The person who does the difficult thing even when nobody will know?
Leader.

Leadership is not loud.
It is not glamorous.

And it is almost never rewarded at the time it occurs.

Why Most Leaders in Organizations Aren't Actually Leaders

Here's a secret you learn after working long enough:

A large percentage of people in leadership roles are not leaders — they're survivors of bureaucracy.

They advanced because they:
- Were politically safe
- Didn't rock the boat
- Agreed with the right people
- Avoided blame
- Smiled in meetings
- Volunteered for "culture initiatives"
- Said yes often enough
- Mastered corporate camouflage

This is not leadership.
This is social navigation.

Organizations reward predictability and loyalty long before they reward competence.

Which is why the people who *should* be leading often aren't — they're too valuable doing the actual work.

D.M. Christensen

Leadership Requires Two Things Schools Rarely Develop

1. Independent Thinking

Not memorization.

Not recitation.

Not fulfilling checklists.

Leaders must be able to look at a situation and see what others don't.

2. Tolerance for Discomfort

Leadership isn't difficult because of complexity.

It's difficult because of fear:
- fear of being wrong
- fear of conflict
- fear of failure
- fear of risk
- fear of judgment

Schools eliminate discomfort.

Leadership requires it.

It's no wonder the pipeline is broken.

The Myth of the "Natural Leader"

Some pretend leadership is innate — something you're either born with or not.

This is wrong.

Nobody exits the womb ready to:
- delegate
- negotiate
- balance budgets
- mitigate risk
- handle stakeholders
- coach weak performers

Leadership is learned.

But the environments we create to teach it are artificial.

Leadership only develops through:
- experience
- mistakes
- pressure
- responsibility
- consequences
- conflict
- reflection

You cannot lecture someone into being a leader.

You can only place them in situations where leadership becomes necessary.

What Real Leadership Looks Like

It looks like:
- Getting the call at 2am and answering it

- Taking responsibility when your team makes a mistake without pointing fingers
- Speaking uncomfortable truths
- Making decisions with incomplete information and owning the consequences
- Staying steady when everyone else loses their mind[2]

Doing the right thing when it is not the easy thing. Real leadership is quiet.

It's often lonely.

And it rarely comes with applause.

Most of it happens behind closed doors, unnoticed, uncelebrated.

That's why so few people truly want it — not the title, but the burden.

The Leadership Mirage

The education system teaches the *image* of leadership.
Corporations reward the *performance* of leadership.
Society praises the *idea* of leadership.

But real leadership — the kind that shapes teams, companies, industries, outcomes, and lives — is far simpler and far harder:

**It is the willingness to step forward when others step back.
Every- Single- Time.**

---

[2] If you can keep your head when all about you
Are losing theirs and blaming it on you (IF by Rudyard Kipling)

It cannot be given.

It cannot be claimed.

It can only be proven.

And no diploma can teach it.

Chapter 6
The Competence Gap

There's a quiet truth most people sense but rarely say aloud:

Many educated people are not competent — they are simply credentialed.

It's not an insult.
It's an observation.
One that becomes painfully clear the moment you leave the bubble of education and enter the workplace.

We live in a world where:
- People with degrees can't write emails.
- Managers can't manage.
- Leaders can't lead.
- Experts can't explain anything without making it sound more complicated than it is.
- Organizations reward confidence more than competence.
- And the loudest person in the room is frequently the least effective.

This is the **competence gap**:

The distance between what people *should* be able to do, given their degrees, and what they can *actually* do.

How the Competence Gap Forms

It isn't mysterious.
It's predictable.

1. Schools reward correctness, not understanding.

Test-taking is largely Memorize → test → forget → repeat.
A GPA doesn't measure capability—it measures short-term memory and compliance to instructors views.

2. Group projects hide incompetence.

Every group has:
- One worker
- One talker
- One ghost
- One excuse-maker
- One person who thinks they're the leader because they made the Google Doc

Schools call this "collaboration."
Employers call it "a sign of things to come."

Reality is it hides the weak and burdens the leader.

3. Theory replaces skill.

Textbooks explain leadership without practical application.

Professors teach business theory without having business experience.

Students graduate fluent in leadership terminology and deficient in leadership experience.

4. Failure is punished, not leveraged.

Real learning requires mistakes.

Schools treat mistakes like moral failures instead of data.

In short:

Traditional education produces people who know *about* things, not people who learn how to *do* things.

The Workplace Makes It Worse

Just as GPA achievement drives student behavior of obedience to instructors, economic reward drives professional behavior. Once graduates enter the professional world, they encounter structures that unintentionally reward incompetence. Notable examples include:

1. Promotion by visibility, not performance

The people who talk the most in meetings aren't always the ones who deliver results.

But visibility is easier to measure than competence.

2. Encouraging blame avoidance disguised as risk management

Employees who take initiative often inherit blame.
Employees who avoid risk often inherit promotions.

3. Using Soft language to hide hard problems

Companies invent phrases like:

- "We need alignment."
- "We need more synergy."
- "We need to rethink our cross-functional bandwidth."

These hold the same meaning:

"No one is doing their job."

But saying it directly would imply accountability.

4. Leadership roles given to the wrong people

Organizations frequently promote:

- The politically safe
- The critical technical expert
- The socially likable
- The unthreatening
- The ones who "fit the culture"

Competence becomes secondary to comfort.

The result?

A structure where capability is optional, but credentials are mandatory.

The Dunning–Kruger Executive Suite

There's a psychological reality behind the competence gap:
- **Incompetent people overestimate their abilities.**
- **Competent people underestimate theirs.**

This is why the least qualified often feel the most confident, and vice versa.

It's also why some executives sound like they're improvising their job description every day.

You've met someone like this:
They can explain nothing clearly, answer nothing directly, and yet speak for ten uninterrupted minutes in a way that makes you wonder whether they're brilliant or just aggressively vague.

Spoiler:
Usually the second one.

Competence Is Rare Because It's Hard

Competence requires:
- Experience
- Discipline
- Repetition
- Humility
- Curiosity
- The ability to say "I don't know"
- The courage to be wrong

- The willingness to do the boring parts of mastery

Most people avoid these.

Not because they're lazy, but because society has taught them that:

1. **Credentials equal competence**
2. **Confidence equals capability**
3. **Complexity equals intelligence**
4. **Busyness equals productivity**

None of these are true.

Competence requires deliberate effort.

Credentials require tuition.

Guess which one is easier to obtain?

Why Competence Matters More Today Than Ever

We live in an era where:

- AI can generate information
- Software automates tasks
- Data is abundant
- Skills become outdated quickly
- Industries evolve faster than degrees

In this environment, competence is no longer "nice to have."

It is a competitive necessity.

Not theoretical capability.

Not textbook fluency.

Not résumé buzzwords.

But **real, demonstrable skill.**

The kind employers can see.
The kind teams rely on.
The kind crises expose.
The kind results reveal.

How to Close the Competence Gap

If you want to become competent — truly competent — the formula is simple, but not easy:

1. Seek problems, not praise.
Competence is forged in responsibility, not recognition.

2. Learn from consequences.
Failure is instruction.
Avoidance is stagnation.

3. Practice with intention.
Repetition without awareness produces habits, not mastery.

4. Build judgment.
Read widely.
Analyze.
Reflect.

Observe. Discuss with experts in the field

Judgment is competence on the inside.
Skill is competence on the outside.

5. Be honest about your weaknesses.

Arrogance protects the ego.
Humility protects your future.

The Competence Gap Is Optional

This chapter isn't a criticism of individuals.
It's a criticism of systems that confuse:

- education with mastery
- participation with understanding
- long hours with effectiveness
- titles with capability
- and credentials with competence

But the gap is optional.
Anyone can close it.
It takes deliberate action — not another degree.

Competence is not a diploma.
It's a decision.

Chapter 7
The Confidence Problem

If the **competence gap** explains why many professionals *can't* do what their jobs require, the **confidence problem** explains why many still believe they can.

Confidence is one of the strangest forces in modern society:

It routinely is promoted over competence, **out-earns intelligence**, and is **out-promoted over skill.**

In fact, if society worked the way résumés suggest it does, we'd see:

- The most qualified people in leadership
- The most capable people making decisions
- The most competent shaping strategy

But we don't.

Instead we see:

- The most confident
- The most technical
- The most vocal
- The most visible
- The least self-aware

Confidence has become currency — sometimes more valuable than ability, preparation, or results. And the market never stops overpaying for it.

Confidence Without Competence

We've all met this person:

- They explain complex things incorrectly
- They speak with authority they didn't earn
- They misinterpret basic information
- They interrupt actual experts
- They never say "I don't know"
- They thrive in job interviews
- They stall in real jobs

This is the person carried upward by **confidence inflation**.

Confidence without competence is like a credit card with no spending limit — impressive at first, catastrophic over time.

It buys titles, promotions, approval, and trust...
right until the moment reality hands them a bill they cannot pay.

Competence Without Confidence

Then there's the opposite group:

- Highly capable
- Deeply knowledgeable
- Thoughtful, precise, detail-oriented
- Rarely self-promoting

- Frequently underestimated
- Often overlooked in meetings
- Trusted by few... yet relied on by everyone

They don't dominate conversations.
They don't oversell themselves.
They don't exaggerate results.
They don't need spotlights.

But here's the tragic part:

Competence is often invisible.
Confidence is often mistaken for competence.

And in environments where perception wins, the quiet expert loses.

Where the Confidence Problem Begins

Confidence is cultivated in childhood and reinforced through the education system.

Overconfidence begins here:

- High-achieving students who never struggled
- Children praised only for talent, not effort
- Participation trophies that reward showing up, not improving
- Teachers who inflate grades to "boost self-esteem"
- Parents who insist their child is a "natural leader" because they talk a lot

Underconfidence begins here:

- Students who learned slowly, but learned thoroughly
- Kids punished for mistakes instead of guided through them
- High performers who never believed they were high performers
- Students who internalized criticism but dismissed praise
- People who equate hesitation with weakness

The system elevates one group and suppresses the other long before adulthood.

By the time both groups enter the workplace:

- The confident overestimate their skill
- The competent underestimate theirs

This is the perfect recipe for mediocrity to rise.

The Corporate Amplifier

Organizations accidentally amplify confidence far more than competence.

Who gets promoted?

Those who *look* ready, not those who *are* ready.

Who leads meetings?

Those who talk the most, not those who know the most.

Who gets visibility?
Those who market themselves, not those who deliver results.

Who succeeds in performance reviews?
Those who frame their year well, not those who performed well.

Who gets opportunities?
Those who ask for them, not those who deserve them.

It's not because corporations want to reward confidence — it's because confidence is easier to evaluate.

Competence requires work to observe.
Confidence announces itself.

The Danger of Unchecked Confidence

There is no problem more destructive to organizations than people who:
1. **Don't know what they're doing,**
2. **Don't know that they don't know, and**
3. **Feel absolutely sure they do.**

These people:
- Overpromise
- Under-deliver
- Miss deadlines
- Avoid accountability
- Escalate risk

- Mislead teams
- Derail projects
- Make decisions that damage organizations

And when results fail, they confidently explain why the failure was:

- Someone else's fault
- A "communication gap"
- A "misalignment of expectations"
- "Not reflective of their leadership style"

Confidence protects egos.
Competence protects outcomes.

Organizations often choose the wrong one.

The Underconfidence Penalty

Equally damaging is how organizations treat capable people who lack confidence.

Highly competent professionals frequently:

- Doubt themselves
- Speak carefully
- Ask clarifying questions
- Understate accomplishments
- Avoid taking credit
- Feel like impostors
- Fear overextending themselves

This creates a paradox:

**The people who should lead often won't,
and the people who shouldn't often will.**

The confidence problem suppresses the very people organizations desperately need.

Confidence ≠ Strength. Competence ≠ Arrogance.

Somewhere along the line, society began confusing categories.

People assume:
- Confidence = strong
- Caution = weak
- Ambition = leadership
- Introversion = lack of initiative
- Loud = right
- Quiet = wrong
- Quick answers = intelligence
- Thoughtful pauses = uncertainty

None of these maps to reality.

True confidence is built on competence.
Arrogance is built on insecurity.
Hesitation is built on thoughtfulness and wisdom.
And real strength is built on the willingness to evaluate oneself honestly.

Unfortunately, honesty and ego rarely share the same room.

Closing the Confidence Gap

The solution is not to eliminate confidence — confidence is valuable. It's to align confidence with competence.

Here's how:

1. Know what you know.

Clarity builds confidence.

2. Know what you don't know.

Humility builds competence.

3. Speak only at the level of your understanding.

Precision builds credibility.

4. Seek feedback from people who aren't afraid to tell you the truth.

Correction builds mastery.

5. Build courage through action, not through affirmation.

Experience builds confidence that lasts.

When confidence grows from competence, it becomes a foundation. When confidence grows without competence, it becomes a liability.

The Confidence Problem Is a Human Problem

This chapter isn't about blaming individuals.
It's about recognizing patterns the modern world reinforces:

- Education rewards correctness, not capability
- Culture rewards visibility, not skill
- Organizations reward boldness, not wisdom
- Society rewards certainty, not accuracy

It's no surprise confidence is broken.

The key is not to eliminate the confident or elevate the insecure — but to build a world where competence matters as much as charisma.

Because the most dangerous combination in any workplace is:

A confident person with nothing to be confident about.

And the most valuable combination is:

A competent person finally confident enough to lead.

Chapter 8
The Illusion of Hard Work

"Work hard."

It's one of society's favorite phrases — embroidered on pillows, printed on posters, shouted by football coaches, whispered by parents, plastered across motivational Instagram feeds, and recited by managers who mistake exhaustion for productivity.

It sounds noble.

It sounds honorable.

It sounds like wisdom distilled through generations.

But here's the truth that makes people uncomfortable:

Hard work is not the problem.
Hard work is the illusion.

The modern world doesn't reward hard work.

It rewards **impact**.

And impact doesn't come from effort — it comes from **effectiveness**.

Hard Work vs. Meaningful Work

There are two kinds of hard work:

1. Productive hard work

Effort that moves you closer to a valued outcome.

2. Performative hard work

Effort that *looks* impressive but accomplishes nothing.

The problem?

Most people — and most companies — cannot tell the difference.

And worse:

They often reward the wrong one.

Why Hard Work Became a Cultural Myth

Hard work once mattered.

In agriculture, manufacturing, construction — labor directly translated into results.

Work more hours, produce more output.

But in today's world — digital, automated, knowledge-driven — effort and outcome are only loosely connected.

You can:

- work a 12-hour day and accomplish little
- work 2 focused hours and solve a major problem

- attend 8 meetings and make zero decisions
- send 50 emails and clarify nothing
- stay late every night and still fail to produce value

Yet society still clings to the nostalgia of labor-based productivity. We've replaced "sweat" with:

- inbox zero
- cc'ing everyone
- Zoom fatigue
- constant notifications
- multi-tasking
- being "always available"

And we call it "working hard."

It isn't.

It's **busyness cosplay.**

Hard Work Has Become a Performance

In many workplaces, "hard work" is not about results — it's about optics.

Employees perform hard work the way actors perform roles:

- arriving early
- staying late
- sighing loudly
- juggling too many tasks
- responding immediately rather than thoughtfully
- walking fast in hallways
- complaining about workload

- holding a laptop at all times

None of this indicates productivity.

It indicates job anxiety mixed with performance art.

Ironically, the people who accomplish the most often **don't look busy**.

They:
- finish work quickly
- simplify processes
- say "no"
- automate tasks
- avoid unnecessary meetings
- focus intensely
- leave on time

This confuses managers who still evaluate employees by facetime rather than outcomes.

The Highest Performers Rarely "Look Busy"

High performers work differently:
- They think before acting.
- They prioritize ruthlessly.
- They protect their focus.
- They solve root problems instead of treating symptoms.
- They rest strategically.
- They optimize systems repeating "the way we do things".
- They don't talk about effort — they deliver results.

To the untrained eye, this can look like laziness.

To anyone who has ever led a high-performing team, it looks like mastery.

The Emotional Addiction to Hard Work

Why does society cling to the illusion?

Because "hard work" provides three emotional rewards:

1. Moral worth

People believe hard work equals virtue.
It doesn't.
Execution does.

2. Predictability

Hard work feels controllable.
Results feel uncertain.

3. Self-justification

If you work hard, you don't have to question whether the work itself matters.

Hard work is comforting.
Effectiveness yields results.

Hard Work Without Strategy Is Just Movement

Consider the hamster wheel.
Lots of effort.
No progress.

Many professionals spend years — even decades — doing the career equivalent:

- answering emails
- refining spreadsheets
- preparing slide decks
- attending recurring meetings
- revising plans
- reviewing the same documents
- "aligning stakeholders"

This activity creates the illusion of importance.
It feels productive because it fills time and people "see" the effort.
But it achieves little.

High performers ask three questions:

1. "Is this necessary?"
2. "Is this the best use of my time?"
3. "Does this move the outcome forward?"

If not, they stop doing it.
Most people don't.
Most people keep doing the "task" because it *feels* like work – it is what school trained them to do .

The Hard Work Trap

The illusion of hard work traps people in cycles that destroy growth:

1. Burnout without progress

Exhaustion mistaken for accomplishment.

2. Doing instead of thinking

Action without strategy.

3. Busyness instead of direction

Movement without trajectory.

4. Effort instead of leverage

Working harder instead of smarter.

5. Rewarding hours instead of value

Paying for time instead of outcomes — a relic of the industrial age.

This is why many hardworking people remain stuck while smarter working and more strategic people accelerate.

The People Who Rise Faster Don't Always Work the Hardest

They aren't the first to arrive or last to leave.
They don't drown in emails.

They aren't overwhelmed.

They rise because they:

- work on the *right* problems
- choose the highest-leverage tasks
- cut out noise
- think clearly
- communicate effectively
- attack issues others avoid
- make thoughtful decisions
- understand systems
- use their time intentionally

Hard work is a tool.
But strategy is the blueprint.

Without the blueprint, the tool is useless.

Why Hard Work Still Feels Necessary

Even though the modern world rewards effectiveness, people cling to hard work because:

- It feels safer
- It feels familiar
- It avoids vulnerability ("I'm working hard!")
- It avoids accountability ("I did everything I could")
- It avoids decision-making ("I'm too busy to think")

Hard work often becomes a shield — protection from the discomfort of stepping back and admitting:

"I'm not sure this is the right thing to be working on."

Effectiveness requires that level of honesty.

Effort does not.

Redefining Hard Work for the Modern World

Hard work still matters — just not the way we were taught.

The new definition is simple:

Hard work = doing the work most people avoid because it requires clarity, judgment, and courage.

Examples:

- Having difficult conversations
- Making decisions without perfect information
- Eliminating your own busy-work
- Saying "no" to distracting tasks
- Taking responsibility when results are unclear
- Focusing intensely when it's easier to multitask
- Resting strategically instead of collapsing
- Learning skills that make you replace your old habits

This is the real hard work.

The work that compounds.

The work that creates results.

D.M. Christensen

The Illusion Ends Here

The truth is this:

The world doesn't reward effort.
It rewards outcomes.

Effort is admirable.
But effort without direction becomes wasteful.

The challenge of the modern era isn't working harder.
It's working intentionally.

Because the most successful people aren't the most exhausted.
They are the most effective.

And the difference between the two is the difference between a life spent running to get somewhere versus a life spent actually getting somewhere.

Chapter 9
The Problem with Teams

Teams are one of the greatest paradoxes of modern work. In theory, they represent:

- collaboration
- shared knowledge
- integrated talent
- diverse viewpoints
- collective intelligence

In practice, they often represent:

- unclear ownership
- uneven workloads
- unnecessary meetings
- conflicting priorities
- personalities in collision
- a constant struggle to decide who's actually in charge

We talk about teams the way people talk about soulmates — as though forming one automatically guarantees synergy, productivity, and "alignment."

But teams don't automatically create greatness or results.

Teams amplify whatever is already there.

If most members are strong, teams enhance performance.
If most people are weak, teams magnify dysfunction.

Either way, a team is not a solution.
It's a multiplier.

Why Teams Rarely Work the Way They Should

Teams fail for predictable reasons — almost all of them structural.

1. No one knows who is actually responsible.

When a task is "shared," it is rarely done.
Because:
- shared responsibility = shared neglect
- collective ownership = no ownership
- group accountability = no accountability

Everyone assumes someone else will handle it.
It is the continuation of "teams" taught in school. This is the birth of mediocrity.

2. Teams are formed to make people feel included, not to get things done.

Modern corporate culture is allergic to excluding people.

So instead of creating small, effective teams, companies form:
- working groups
- task forces
- tiger teams
- pods
- councils
- committees

Anything to avoid saying, "We only need three people to do this."

3. Meetings replace actual work.

There is no organizational dysfunction more widespread than this:

Teams spend more time talking about work than doing work.

You've sat in these meetings:
- two people contribute
- four people spectate
- one person dominates
- everyone loses time

A one-hour meeting of eight people is not one hour. It is eight hours – a full day - of productivity burned.

4. Personalities overshadow purpose.

The reality of team dynamics often looks like this:
- The loud person wins
- The agreeable person gets overworked
- The thoughtful person gets ignored

- The insecure person slows progress
- The passive person avoids conflict
- The ambitious person takes credit

Teams rarely fail because of skill.
They fail because of behavior.

The Myth of "Collaboration"

Organizations fetishize collaboration and rarely understand what it means.

Collaboration is not:
- constant communication
- group brainstorming
- collective decision-making
- aligning every detail
- sitting through endless Zoom sessions

Collaboration is:
- clarity of purpose
- shared direction
- complimentary skills
- rapid information flow
- trust
- speed

Collaboration is *coordination*, not *committee*.

The moment collaboration becomes a substitute for decisiveness, the team stops performing.

Why Teams Slow Down High Performers

Every high performer knows this feeling:

You could do the task in 30 minutes.
The team will take two weeks.

Not because they're incompetent — but because teams introduce friction:

- negotiation
- miscommunication
- dependency
- compromise
- diverse priorities
- approval loops
- the need to make everyone comfortable

High performers prefer clarity, autonomy, and speed.

Teams prefer consensus, discussion, and process.

This creates a permanent tension:

the people capable of delivering results the fastest are slowed by the system designed to "support" them.

The Hidden Burden Placed on Capable People

In nearly every team, 20% of people carry 80% of the work.

These individuals:

- take ownership

- clean up mistakes
- anticipate problems
- understand the whole system
- become the default problem-solvers
- carry invisible emotional and operational weight

Meanwhile, others contribute far less while receiving equal credit.

This is why high performers often resent teamwork — not because they dislike people, but because they dislike inefficiency and imbalance.

The Leadership Mistake: Confusing Harmony with Health

Many leaders misinterpret harmony as success.

A team that:

- never argues
- agrees on everything
- smiles a lot
- avoids conflict
- praises each other constantly

...is not necessarily a healthy team.

It might be a conflict-avoidant team.
It might be a passive team.
It might be a complacent team.

Healthy teams challenge one another — respectfully but honestly.

If there is no friction, there is no growth.

The Only Two Questions That Make Teams Work

High-functioning teams ask — and answer — two questions clearly:

1. Who owns what?

Not: "We own this."
But: "*You* own this. *I* own that."

Ownership creates momentum.

2. What decision-making authority does each person have?

If people can't decide, they can't execute.

Ambiguity kills speed.
Speed kills dysfunction.

When teams fail, it is almost always because these two questions were never resolved.

The Team Size Rule That Fixes Everything

Amazon famously used the "two-pizza rule":

If a team cannot be fed with two pizzas, it is too big.

Why?

Because:

- communication collapses
- accountability disperses
- decisions slow
- politics rise
- coordination becomes complex

Teams perform best when they are:

- small
- skilled
- empowered
- aligned
- decisive
- trusted

Everything else is just noise.

What Great Teams Actually Look Like

They are not defined by friendliness.
Or enthusiasm.
Or how often they meet.
Or how well they "collaborate."

Great teams:

- argue about ideas
- agree on goals
- trust each other's competence
- resolve conflict quickly

- communicate clearly
- own their work
- expect excellence
- move fast
- deliver

These teams are rare because they require two ingredients that organizations struggle with:

1. **Competent people**
2. **Leaders who can remove obstacles instead of creating them**

Teams Don't Make People Better — People Make Teams Better

The modern workplace treats teams as a magic cure-all.
But the truth is simpler:

Strong individuals make strong teams.
Weak individuals make weak teams.

A team is not a strategy.
It is a structure.

What matters is who's in it, what they're empowered to do, and whether they're allowed to operate without drowning in unnecessary processes.

When teams work, they are extraordinary.
When they don't, they drain time, talent, and energy from the people who could succeed without them.

Chapter 10
Why Good Systems Beat Good People

Most organizations believe their success depends on hiring "the best people."

It's a comforting idea — almost romantic.

But it's also wrong.

Good people matter.
But good systems matter more.

In fact, if you look closely at the most effective organizations—across business, government, health, technology, or the military—one pattern emerges:

Average people inside good systems outperform great people inside broken systems.

This is the opposite of what most leaders want to hear.

But it's the truth.

The Myth of the "Rockstar Employee"

Every company fantasizes about finding "rockstars":

- the genius
- the visionary
- the brilliant strategist
- the natural leader
- the irreplaceable problem-solver

The problem?

Rockstars are rare, expensive, difficult to retain, and impossible to scale.

Worse, organizations often expect rockstars to succeed **in spite of**:

- poor communication
- unclear priorities
- chaotic reporting structures
- redundant processes
- political landmines
- constant reorganization
- outdated tools
- unrealistic timelines

And when those stars fail, the system blames the individual instead of the environment.

It's like hiring a world-class chef and asking them to cook in a kitchen with no stove, broken utensils, and a fridge full of expired ingredients.

The failure isn't the chef.
It's the system.

Systems Are Multipliers

A system is:

- a set of processes
- a set of expectations
- a structure of incentives
- a distribution of authority
- a flow of information
- a cultural pattern
- a method of decision-making

When systems work, people flourish.

When systems fail, people struggle.

A good system makes average people look exceptional.
A bad system makes exceptional people look average.

This is why so many high performers thrive in one company and fail in another.

It's not the person.
It's the environment.

What Broken Systems Look Like

Broken systems share predictable symptoms:

1. No clarity of ownership

Everyone is responsible = no one is responsible.

2. Constant firefighting

Every problem becomes urgent because nothing is addressed early.

3. Decision paralysis

No one knows who can say "yes," so everyone waits.

4. Communication chaos

Information is lost, duplicated, or distorted.

5. Incentives that reward the wrong behaviors

Activity instead of results.

Visibility instead of outcomes.

Politics instead of performance.

6. Tools chosen for aesthetics, not function

Fancy dashboards.

Pretty workflows.

Zero impact.

7. "Hero culture"

The same few people fix everything — until they burn out.

These are not people problems.

They are system problems.

Fixing individuals won't fix systemic failure.

Fixing the system will fix individual performance.

Why Leaders Misunderstand Systems

Many leaders confuse people problems with system problems because:

1. Systems are invisible when they're working.

They only become visible when they break.

2. People are easier to blame than structures.

It's simple to say:
"Why didn't John do this right?"
It's harder to ask:
"Why did the system allow this to happen?"

3. Leaders overestimate their influence.

They believe their personality or style can compensate for broken processes.
It can't.

4. It requires humility to admit the structure is flawed.

Humility is rare in leadership.

5. Fixing systems takes patience and discipline.

Firing someone is quicker.

Why Good People Struggle in Bad Systems

Talented individuals often become frustrated, disengaged, or even ineffective inside poorly designed systems.

Because even the best people can't overcome:

- unclear priorities
- messy handoffs
- conflicting expectations
- poor documentation
- slow decisions
- low trust
- weak leadership
- lack of resources
- constant rework

A high performer can create excellence — but only within the boundaries of the system they operate in.

Systems set limits.
People operate inside those limits.

Why Average People Thrive in Good Systems

Well-designed systems:

- clarify roles
- reduce friction
- streamline communication
- protect focus
- prevent duplication

- guide decisions
- maintain accountability
- reduce cognitive load
- eliminate ambiguity

This allows even average individuals to perform above expectations.

Because systems don't rely on talent.
They rely on structure.

They remove complexity so people can succeed without heroics.

This is why:

- McDonald's can hire teenagers and still run smoothly
- airlines can operate globally with predictable workflows
- the military can train millions of recruits to a minimum standard
- great franchises replicate excellence across locations

The system does the heavy lifting.
The people follow it.

The Three Components of Effective Systems

A high-functioning system has three ingredients:

1. Clear ownership

Every task, decision, and outcome has a name attached to it.

No committees.
No shared responsibility.
No "team owns this."

One person.

Clear accountability.

2. Simple, repeatable processes

Complexity is the enemy of execution.

The best systems are:

- easy to understand
- easy to follow
- easy to train
- easy to troubleshoot
- easy to scale

If a process requires a 40-page manual to explain, it will fail.

3. Fast, unambiguous decision-making

Speed is a competitive advantage.

Great systems define:

- who decides
- how fast they must decide
- what information they need
- what authority they have
- what happens next

Slow decisions kill momentum.

Momentum is everything.

The Systems Approach to Leadership

Leaders who understand systems focus on:

- designing workflows
- removing obstacles
- streamlining decisions
- eliminating dependencies
- documenting processes
- aligning incentives
- ensuring clarity
- measuring outcomes

They do not focus on micromanaging individuals.

Micromanagement is a symptom of weak systems.

Empowerment is a symptom of strong systems.

Systems Scale. People Don't.

This is the secret many leaders never learn:

People do not scale. Systems do.

If success depends on "great people," your organization is fragile.
If success depends on "great systems," your organization is resilient.

This is why mediocre companies collapse when key individuals leave...

...and great companies remain strong regardless of turnover.

Systems create stability.
People create variability.

The best organizations use both — but build on systems first.

The Hard Truth

If your organization is:

- slow
- political
- chaotic
- unclear
- frustrating
- repetitive
- inconsistent

...it is because your **systems** are slow, political, chaotic, unclear, frustrating, repetitive, and inconsistent.

Fix the system, and the people will improve.

Fix the people, and the system will break again next quarter.

Good Systems Beat Good People

Not because people don't matter.
Not because talent isn't real.
Not because individuals can't drive greatness.

But because systems:

- enable
- support
- empower

- absorb mistakes
- reduce friction
- amplify ability
- protect progress

Systems lift people higher than effort alone ever could.

In a world obsessed with talent, the organizations that win are the ones obsessed with structure.

Because at the end of the day:

A good person inside a bad system will fail.
A decent person inside a great system will thrive.
And a great person inside a great system will change everything.

Chapter 11
The Myth of the Natural Leader

Leadership is often treated as a genetic trait — something you're born with, like eye color or lactose intolerance. People love the idea of the "natural leader": a charismatic figure who emerges from childhood with the innate ability to influence, inspire, and command a room.

It's a romantic story.

It's also entirely wrong.

There is no "leadership gene."
There is no instinctive leadership reflex.
There is only **skill**, **behavior**, and **experience**.

Yet society continues to believe in the myth because it absolves people from doing the work required to *become* leaders.

If leadership is innate, then:

- You either have it or you don't.
- Organizations don't need to train it.
- Schools don't need to develop it.
- People don't need to cultivate it.

It's an appealing shortcut — one that excuses underdevelopment and masks incompetence.

But real leadership does not appear instinctively.
It is **forged**, not **inherited.**

Why the Myth Exists

The myth survives for three reasons:

1. Confusing personality with leadership

Certain personalities *look* like leaders:

- confident
- extroverted
- articulate
- decisive
- charismatic
- commanding
- socially skilled

But these traits are not leadership — they are **presentation**.

You can speak well and still be wrong.
You can be charismatic and still be incompetent.
You can be extroverted and still make poor decisions.

Leadership is not how you talk.
Leadership is what you *do*.

2. Mistaking early dominance for potential

Children who talk first, argue boldly, or assume authority in group projects are often labeled "future leaders."

In reality, these behaviors can also indicate:

- impatience
- insecurity
- impulsiveness
- controlling tendencies
- the desire to dominate rather than collaborate

Yet schools and parents frequently reward these traits instead of shaping them.

This creates the illusion that leadership is something exhibited early — when in reality it's something learned slowly.

3. Retrospective storytelling

When someone becomes successful, we rewrite their past:

- "They were always a leader."
- "They were born for this."
- "They've always had 'it.'"

But this is hindsight bias.

Success feels inevitable only after it happens.

If you rewind their life story, you'll often see:

- failures
- uncertainty
- mistakes

- growth spurts
- mentors
- hard lessons
- painful experiences
- deliberate skill-building

Natural leaders aren't natural.

They're **developed**, then mythologized.

Leadership Is a Learned Skill Set

Leadership is not one thing.

It is a *collection* of things — competencies anyone can learn:

- communication
- decision-making
- emotional regulation
- judgment
- strategic thinking
- conflict navigation
- accountability
- empathy
- resilience
- influence
- time management
- adaptability

Not a single item on this list comes pre-installed at birth.

Leadership is like language:

everyone has the capacity for it,

but fluency requires practice.

Experience Shapes Leaders — Not Personality

Most strong leaders share the same developmental experiences:

- they failed early
- they took responsibility when young
- they were forced into uncomfortable situations
- they solved problems alone
- they learned from consequences
- they adapted to change
- they dealt with difficult people
- they held roles with real accountability
- they mastered a skill deeply before leading others

These experiences produce maturity and clarity — not ego or theatrics.

Real leadership does not emerge from comfort.
It emerges from **responsibility**.

Why the Myth Is Dangerous

Believing leadership is innate has consequences.

1. Organizations misidentify leaders

They promote:

- charisma over competence
- extroversion over judgment
- confidence over capability

- presentation over performance

And then wonder why morale collapses.

2. High-potential individuals underestimate themselves

Quiet, thoughtful, capable people often assume:

"I'm not a natural leader."

Translation:

"No one told me I looked like one."

These individuals — who often have superior judgment — never pursue leadership roles because they've been conditioned to believe they lack the "leadership personality."

This is a loss for them, and a disaster for organizations.

3. Bad leaders avoid accountability

If leadership is innate, then failure isn't their fault — it's simply "who they are."

The myth becomes a shield that protects ego and excuses incompetence.

4. Organizations avoid doing the hard work of developing leaders

Why train leadership if you can simply "hire naturals"?

Because naturals don't exist.

And hope is not a strategy.

Natural Leaders Aren't Leaders — They're Early Talkers

Most people labeled "natural leaders" in childhood share the same traits:
- they speak quickly
- they speak confidently
- they speak often

This is not leadership.
This is verbal enthusiasm.

Leadership requires:
- discipline
- clarity
- courage
- patience
- perspective
- humility

These traits almost always develop later — rarely in childhood, and rarely through flattery.

The Qualities Real Leaders Develop Over Time

There are traits almost every great leader has — and they are always learned:

1. Calm under pressure

You learn calmness by surviving chaos.

2. Sound judgment

You develop judgment by making real decisions with real consequences.

3. Objectivity

You gain objectivity by recognizing your own bias.

4. Accountability

You learn accountability by owning failure.

5. Clarity

Clarity comes from experience and discipline, not personality.

6. Influence

Influence is earned — slowly — and through consistency.

7. Empathy

Not "niceness," but the ability to understand what people need from you.

8. Vision

Vision is the product of exposure, curiosity, and deep thinking — not natural brilliance.

Leadership is not magic.

It is not charisma.

It is not destiny.

It is maturity, built intentionally.

The Myth Is Comfortable — Reality Is Harder

The myth of the natural leader gives people the illusion of simplicity:

- either you have "it"
- or you never will

It creates clarity, but false clarity.

Real leadership development is slower, less glamorous, and more personal:

- continuous practice
- deliberate discomfort
- the willingness to change
- the courage to confront your own weaknesses

It's messy.

It's unromantic.

It's work.

But it is work that anyone can do.

You Don't Need to Be Born a Leader — You Need to Choose to Become One

The truth is simple:

Leadership is not a gift you inherit.
It is a responsibility you step into.

Some step in earlier.
Some step in later.
Some need more practice.
Some need more pressure.
Some need the right mentor.
Some need the right moment.

But everyone can become a leader.

The myth says leadership belongs to a chosen few.

Reality shows leadership belongs to anyone who is willing to grow.

And that is far more powerful than any myth could ever be.

Chapter 12
The Illusion of Communication

If you ask any organization what its biggest challenge is, you'll hear the same answer nearly every time:

"Communication."

It's the universal scapegoat — the explanation offered for failures, delays, frustration, and confusion.
It's safe.
It's vague.
It offends no one.
It solves nothing.

"Communication" has become a corporate placeholder for:
- misalignment
- unclear ownership
- poor and diffused decisions
- weak leadership
- lack of process
- missing expectations

- conflicting priorities
- silence at the wrong moments

But instead of admitting these deeper issues, people blame communication — as if the problem is simply that words didn't float through the air properly.

Communication isn't a problem.
It's the symptom of deeper problems.

Why People Think Communication Is the Issue

Because on the surface, it *looks* like it:
- Someone didn't update someone else
- A message wasn't clear
- A detail was missed
- A meeting was misunderstood
- A task wasn't documented
- An email went unread
- Assumptions were made
- A conversation was avoided

It's easy to conclude:

"If we communicated better, this wouldn't happen."

But most "communication failures" occur *after* the real failure happens.

And the real failure is almost always structural.

What People Call a Communication Problem Is Usually Something Else

Here are the actual causes behind most communication issues:

1. Lack of ownership

If no one knows who owns a task, no one highlights the problems and communicates them.

Ownership creates communication.
Ambiguity destroys it.

2. Unclear decision-making authority

When people don't know who decides, they either:
- wait
- escalate
- talk in circles
- or generally avoid the topic

This gets mislabeled as "communication."

It's actually indecision or unwillingness to own responsibility.

3. Poor processes

If the workflow is broken, communication becomes firefighting.

People become messengers instead of contributors.

4. Misaligned incentives

When priorities differ, communication becomes distorted:

- People hide information to protect themselves.
- People exaggerate their problems to avoid ownership.
- People defend their work to direct fault elsewhere.
- People downplay issues to highlight their contribution.

This isn't communication failure.

It's incentive failure.

5. Lack of trust

Where trust is low:

- people filter their responses
- people soften truths
- people hesitate to avoid disagreements
- people avoid conflict

And then blame "communication."

6. No shared context

If two people don't understand the situation in the same way, even perfect communication won't help.

This is a context problem, not a communication problem.

The Communication Paradox

Here's the irony:

Organizations communicate more today than ever before — and understand each other less.

Why?

Because organizations confuse volume with clarity.

They produce:

- more messages
- more emails
- more meetings
- more threads
- more notifications
- more documents
- more "visibility"
- more dashboards

The increase in communication quantity creates the illusion that information is flowing.

But **information is not communication.**

And communication is not alignment.

The Meeting Illusion

Many companies use meetings to compensate for structural confusion. When clarity is low, meetings increase — not because they are needed, but because no one knows what's going on.

Meetings become therapy:

- reassurance
- emotional safety
- the illusion of progress
- collective avoidance of responsibility

Every unnecessary meeting is a structural signal that something upstream is broken.

The Email Illusion of "Communication"

People believe their job is to "keep everyone updated."

This creates inboxes full of:

- CCs that no one reads
- long threads masking simple decisions
- performative documentation
- vague recaps
- pointless FYIs
- status updates with no status

Email is not communication.
It is a container of words.

What matters is the content, not the container.

The Clarity Principle

There is one rule that solves most communication problems:

Clarity creates communication.

Communication does not create clarity.

If roles, goals, decisions, and priorities are clear, communication flows naturally.

If roles, goals, decisions, and priorities are unclear, no amount of talking will fix it.

Why Communication Is Emotionally Charged

Communication becomes difficult when emotions enter the equation:
- fear
- insecurity
- ego
- defensiveness
- avoidance
- resentment
- politics
- uncertainty

People don't struggle to communicate facts.
They struggle to communicate feelings.

That's why "communication problems" often appear in environments where people:
- don't feel safe speaking honestly
- don't want to be blamed
- don't trust leadership
- are afraid to challenge decisions
- are conditioned to agree publicly and disagree privately

These are emotional issues, not informational ones.

What Real Communication Looks Like

Real communication is:

- clear
- simple
- direct
- timely
- honest
- relevant
- action-oriented

Not long.

Not loud.

Not constant.

Real communication sounds like:

- "I own this."
- "You decide."
- "This is the priority."
- "This is the deadline."
- "Here's what's unclear."
- "Here's the risk."
- "Here's the next step."

Anything more complicated is noise disguised as communication.

Why Good Teams Communicate Less, Not More

High-performing teams aren't chatty.
They're aligned.

They don't need:
- constant updates
- frequent check-ins
- detailed reports
- redundant meetings

Because:
- roles are clear
- expectations are shared
- goals are understood
- trust is high
- decisions are fast
- accountability is visible

Communication becomes effortless — because process and systems do the heavy lifting.

The Miscommunication Loop

When communication is unclear, people overcommunicate.
When people overcommunicate, clarity decreases.

This is why organizations spin endlessly in:

1. Confusion

2. Over-explaining
3. Misinterpretation
4. More confusion
5. More communication
6. Still no alignment

It's not the amount of communication that matters — it's the **quality and structure** underlying it.

Fix the System, Not the Messaging

Most communication training focuses on:

- tone
- delivery
- messaging
- feedback style
- meeting etiquette

These things help — a little.
But they do not fix the root cause.

Communication problems disappear when organizations fix:

- ownership
- priorities
- decision authority
- documentation
- incentives
- trust
- emotional safety
- process design

Communication is a lagging indicator of process and structural health.

It improves automatically when the process and structure does.

The Illusion Ends Here

Communication is not a magic skill that can repair broken systems, dysfunctional leadership, unclear processes, or cultural dysfunction.

It is the *result* of a healthy system — not the cause.

The truth is simple:

If your structure is clear, your communication will be clear.
If your structure is confused, your communication will be confused.

Better communication is not the solution.
Better systems are.

Because communication is not the problem.
It is the mirror.

And it faithfully reflects whatever the organization truly is.

Chapter 13
The Incentive Problem

If you want to understand why people behave the way they do — in organizations, in politics, in schools, in any system — you only need to understand one rule:

People respond to incentives.
Not intentions.
Not mission statements.
Not values posters hanging in hallways.
Incentives.

Incentives shape behavior more powerfully than talent, culture, personality, or leadership philosophy. They are invisible strings that guide actions, decisions, and priorities.

Everything you see — good or bad — emerges from incentives.

If you want to change behavior,
you change incentives.
If you don't,
you won't.

It's that simple.

It's that uncomfortable.

Why The Incentive Problem Is So Common

Organizations rarely design incentives intentionally.

They grow accidentally — shaped by:

- legacy culture – "the way we've always done it"
- outdated processes
- personalities in leadership
- political pressure
- emotional comfort
- unexamined habits

The result?

Systems unintentionally incentivize:

- mediocrity
- avoidance
- blame
- bureaucracy
- silence
- short-termism
- risk aversion

And then leadership wonders:

"Why don't people take initiative?"

The incentives reward safety and punishes initiative.

D.M. Christensen

The Two Types of Incentives

Every environment contains both explicit and implicit incentives.

1. Explicit Incentives

These are written down:

- compensation
- bonuses
- promotions
- performance evaluations
- KPIs
- job descriptions

Explicit incentives tell you what the organization *claims* to value.

2. Implicit Incentives

These are not written down — they're observed:

- who gets rewarded
- who gets ignored
- who gets promoted
- who gets blamed
- who gets protected
- how decisions are made
- how mistakes are treated
- how conflict is handled
- what leaders tolerate

Implicit incentives tell you what the organization **actually** values.

And the gap between the two determines morale.

When Explicit and Implicit Incentives Clash

This is where dysfunction grows.

For example:

Explicit: "We value innovation."

Implicit: "If your idea fails, your career suffers."

Result:

No innovation.

Explicit: "We reward initiative."

Implicit: "If you work outside your role and step on toes, you get reprimanded."

Result:

No initiative.

Explicit: "We believe in honesty."

Implicit: "We punish bad news."

Result:

Everyone lies through selective optimism.

Explicit: "We want cross-functional collaboration."

Implicit: "We promote people who outperform other teams."

Result:

Territorial behavior increases.

Explicit: "We value efficiency."

Implicit: "We reward people who look busy."

Result:

Performative work explodes.

Explicit: "We want long-term thinking."

Implicit: "We evaluate quarterly metrics."

Result:

Short-termism dominates.

When explicit and implicit incentives diverge, implicit incentives always win.

People follow results, not slogans.

The Incentive–Behavior Loop

The loop is simple:

1. **Incentives** shape behavior
2. **Behavior** shapes outcomes
3. **Outcomes** reinforce incentives

This loop continues until:

- the system collapses

- the incentives are redesigned
- or leadership changes

Most leaders try to change behavior directly.
But behavior follows incentives.

If you want people to do something different,
you must reward something different.

Why Bad Incentives Create Good Intentions with Bad Outcomes

Most dysfunctional behavior in organizations is not malicious.
It's logical.

For example:
- If you reward avoiding mistakes → people hide problems.
- If you reward hitting metrics → people manipulate metrics.
- If you reward heroic firefighting → people ignore prevention.
- If you reward alignment → people avoid conflict.
- If you reward agreement → people silence themselves.
- If you reward speed → quality drops.
- If you reward perfection → progress slows.

People adapt to the environment they are in — even if the environment is destructive.

It's not about ethics.
It's about incentives.

The Moral Illusion

When people behave poorly at work, leaders often blame:

- character
- motivation
- judgment
- laziness

But these are symptoms.

The cause is always deeper.

Human behavior is not moral —
it's Darwinian.

It follows patterns created by the system.

If the system rewards dysfunction,
you get dysfunction.

If the system rewards excellence,
you get excellence.

It has nothing to do with people being "good" or "bad."

Why Incentives Matter More Than Talent

Talent is individual.
Incentives are structural.

Talent accelerates when incentives align.
Talent withers when incentives conflict.

This is why:

- talented people quit
- experienced people disengage
- ambitious people shrink
- thoughtful people stay silent
- high performers burn out
- leaders become ineffective

Not because they lack ability.
Because their environment lacks support.

Incentives decide whether talent becomes value or becomes frustration.

The Most Common Organizational Incentive Problems

1. Rewarding busyness instead of results

People who appear busy win.
People who finish work quickly lose.

2. Rewarding political skill over competence

Visibility outweighs value.

3. Rewarding consensus over truth

Groupthink replaces clarity.

4. Rewarding crisis response over prevention

Hero culture replaces planning.

5. Rewarding agreement over honesty

The truth becomes a risk.

6. Rewarding perfection over progress

Everything slows to protect egos.

7. Rewarding individual achievement over team success

Internal competition destroys collaboration.

None of these problems stem from people.
They stem from incentives.

The Hidden Power of Removing Bad Incentives

Here's a leadership secret few understand:

You don't always need to add better incentives.
You often just need to remove bad ones.

For example:
- remove the punishment for failure → people innovate
- remove the reward for busyness → people prioritize
- remove the punishment for honesty → people communicate

- remove the reward for politics → people collaborate
- remove the punishment for risk → people innovate
- remove the reward for firefighting → people prevent problems

When you remove the wrong incentives,
the right behaviors emerge naturally.

This is how high-performing cultures are actually built.

Great Cultures Aren't Built — They Are Designed

Leaders often think culture is intangible.

It isn't.

Culture is the cumulative result of what a system rewards and punishes.

A healthy culture emerges when:
- incentives support long-term success
- performance is measured clearly
- ownership is defined
- accountability is balanced
- good behavior is recognized
- destructive behavior is corrected
- trust is maintained

Culture is not a mystery.
It is a series of cause-and-effect relationships that compound over time.

And the engine behind every culture is the incentive structure.

The Hard Truth

If you want to understand any organization, ask one question:

"What does this environment reward?"

The answer will tell you everything:

- how people behave
- how teams function
- how decisions are made
- how leaders operate
- how results happen
- how problems develop
- how success is created or destroyed

If you ever want to transform an organization,
you don't need slogans.
You don't need speeches.
You don't need motivational posters.

You need to redesign the incentives.

Because people don't follow vision.
People don't follow values.
People don't follow strategy.

People follow incentives.
Every. Single. Time.

Chapter 14
The Failure of Modern Management

If you ask people what management is supposed to do, you'll get answers like:

- "support the team"
- "remove obstacles"
- "provide direction"
- "develop talent"
- "make decisions"
- "ensure alignment"
- "drive results"

These answers are correct.

But they rarely describe the reality.

Because modern management — in many organizations — doesn't manage.

It supervises.

It monitors.

It reports.

It performs.

Management has become a shadow of what it was designed to be.

Not because managers are bad people, but because the **role itself has been corrupted by structure, incentives, and culture**.

Management didn't fail because individuals failed.
Management failed because the environment changed — and the role didn't.

Where Management Went Wrong

The world of work transformed dramatically over the past several decades:

- industries evolved
- technology exploded
- knowledge work replaced manual labor
- teams became distributed
- decisions accelerated
- complexity multiplied

But management practices did not evolve with the work.

They remained rooted in old industrial logic reinforced by our educational system:

- control
- oversight
- process enforcement
- hierarchy
- compliance

This legacy thinking is why "management" often feels like bureaucracy instead of leadership.

The Illusion of Oversight

A dangerous assumption exists in modern organizations:

More oversight = better outcomes.

This has never been true.

Oversight creates:

- delays
- bottlenecks
- unnecessary approvals
- fear of independence
- diminished creativity
- reduced ownership

Yet many managers believe their value comes from:

- monitoring
- reviewing
- approving
- policing
- validating
- coordinating
- "being in the loop"

This mindset creates dependency —
not performance.

Oversight is not leadership.

It's management theater.

Management Has Become Too Upward-Facing

Modern managers spend most of their time doing something their teams never see:

managing up.

They prepare:

- status updates
- slides
- dashboards
- reports
- forecasts
- summaries
- pre-meeting documents
- post-meeting documents
- "alignment briefs"
- "visibility memos"

Managers today often communicate more with *their bosses* than with their own teams.

This reverses the function of management.

They are supposed to support the team.
Instead, they support the structure above them.

The result?

Teams become under-led.

Organizations become over-managed.

Management Has Been Confused with Busyness

Many managers believe that to justify their role they must appear constantly involved.

So they:

- schedule meetings
- request updates
- check in frequently
- ask for rewrites
- add process steps
- ask for "alignment"
- request more data
- create dashboards no one uses

This activity feels like contribution.
But it isn't.

Managers mistake **activity** for **value**.

It's the same illusion as a toddler waving their arms and calling it exercise.

The Decision-Making Crisis

The number one failure of modern management is the inability to make decisions.

Managers today:

- overanalyze
- escalate unnecessarily
- defer to committees
- delay for more data
- avoid risk
- fear being wrong
- fear being blamed
- fear stepping on toes
- fear acting without permission

So decisions stagnate.

Projects stall.
Teams lose momentum.
Problems grow.
Morale erodes.

A manager who cannot make decisions is not a manager.
They are a coordinator.

And coordinators do not drive results.

The Risk Aversion Spiral

Modern organizations punish mistakes more than inaction.

This creates a predictable pattern:

- Managers avoid risk
- Managers avoid bold decisions
- Managers avoid accountability

- Managers avoid telling the truth
- Managers avoid challenging leadership
- Managers avoid conflict

Risk aversion becomes cultural.

And when nobody will take risks…
nobody can lead.

Managers Are Overloaded with the Wrong Responsibilities

Most managers today are trapped between two incompatible expectations:

Expectation 1:
"Lead your team."

Expectation 2:
"Follow every rule, process, checklist, and policy without deviation."

You cannot lead while being micromanaged from above.
This contradiction leaves managers stuck in the middle, unable to satisfy either side.

Management becomes less about leadership
and more about survival.

The Emotional Cost of Bad Management Systems

When systems are broken, managers inherit the emotional burden:
- fixing others' mistakes
- calming frustrated team members
- absorbing pressure from above – "providing air cover"
- mediating conflicts
- compensating for poor decisions
- maintaining morale amid dysfunction

This emotional labor is invisible in performance reviews, but overwhelming in reality.

Most managers burn out not from workload — but from contradiction.

The Competence Gap at the Management Level

Many people become managers not because they are leaders, but because:
- it was the only path to promotion
- they had seniority
- they were politically aligned
- they stayed long enough
- they were the only option
- they were slightly less bad than others

As a result:

The average manager is not a leader.

They are a promoted individual contributor.

And the skill set does not translate.

Management requires:
- communication
- clarity
- judgment
- prioritization
- coaching
- conflict handling
- delegation
- emotional intelligence
- decision-making

But many new managers only know how to do the work they used to do —

and now must learn leadership in real time, under pressure, with little support.

The Accountability Illusion

In many organizations, accountability flows *downward* but not *upward*.

Teams are held accountable.
Managers are not.

This creates cultures where:
- managers hide behind their teams
- poor leadership goes unaddressed
- teams weaken while managers remain

- talent leaves while dysfunction stays

Accountability must flow both ways.
Without it, leadership decays.

The Three Functions Management Is *Supposed* to Serve

True management — the kind that produces strong teams — fulfills only three responsibilities:

1. Create clarity

Teams need to know:
- what matters
- why it matters
- what success looks like
- who owns what
- how decisions are made

Without clarity, people drown in uncertainty.

2. Remove obstacles

Managers must clear the path, not clutter it.

That means:
- eliminating ambiguity
- simplifying processes
- accelerating decisions
- protecting focus

- resolving conflict
- securing resources

Leadership is subtraction, not addition.

3. Develop people

The true measure of a leader is the quality of their team.

Not:
- how busy they are
- how many meetings they attend
- how much reporting they do

But:
- how capable their people become
- how confident their people are
- how independently their people operate
- how effectively their team functions without them

Great managers build people
so their people no longer depend on them.

Why Modern Management Fails

Because managers today are:
- incentivized incorrectly
- overwhelmed structurally
- misaligned culturally
- unsupported organizationally
- untrained behaviorally

- punished for leading
- rewarded for performing
- trapped in bureaucracy

Management is failing because the *process* is failing — not the individuals.

Fix the process, and managers rise.
Keep the process broken, and managers sink.

The Hard Truth

Most management failures stem from one simple reality:

The system asks managers to control people instead of empower them.

When leadership becomes supervision,
teams weaken.
When leadership becomes performance,
results suffer.
When leadership becomes bureaucracy,
people disengage.

The true purpose of management is not oversight.

It is:

- clarity
- protection
- guidance
- decision

- development
- empowerment

Real management elevates people.

Modern management often suffocates them.

Chapter 15
Why Competence Feels Threatening

Most people say they appreciate competence.

They *think* they want:
- smart colleagues
- capable managers
- efficient teams
- high performers
- clear thinkers
- strong leaders

But in practice, competence makes people uncomfortable.

Not because competence is aggressive,
but because competence is **revealing**.

Competence exposes:
- laziness
- insecurity
- excuses
- inconsistency

- fragility
- incompetence in others

And people don't like being exposed.

In many environments, competence is not admired.
It is resented.

Not because others want failure —
but because competence disrupts the comfortable equilibrium of mediocrity.

Competence Creates Contrast

Human beings measure themselves through comparison.

When someone more capable shows up, it creates contrast.
And contrast creates discomfort:

- "Why are they so fast?"
- "Why are they so confident?"
- "Why do they see things I don't?"
- "Why do they produce more with less effort?"
- "Why does everyone rely on them?"

Even if no one says these things out loud, they feel them.

Competence becomes a mirror —
and most people don't enjoy seeing themselves in high definition.

Competence Exposes Incompetence

In weak cultures, competence is treated like a threat because it:
- raises standards
- highlights inefficiencies
- disrupts comfortable routines
- reveals poor decision-making
- challenges outdated assumptions
- pressures others to improve

People who have gotten away with mediocrity do not want the bar raised.

People who have been "just good enough" do not want excellence next to them.

In dysfunctional environments, competence is destabilizing.

Competence Removes Excuses

Many people rely on excuses to maintain emotional comfort:
- "It's too hard."
- "It takes too long."
- "No one can do it that fast."
- "That's just how it works here."
- "We've tried that."
- "Leadership won't allow it."

Then a competent person arrives and proves every excuse wrong.

Now the team has a dilemma:

Either acknowledge the new standard...
or resent the person who set it.

Guess which one happens more often?

Competence Changes Power Dynamics

Power in organizations is often based on perception — not actual capability.

Competence threatens people who rely on:
- visibility
- charisma
- politics
- networking
- tenure
- personality
- appearance of busyness

Competence is dangerous because it shifts influence away from:
- talkers
- performers
- manipulators
- weak leaders

...and toward people who can actually deliver results.

That makes insecure people feel exposed and endangered.

Competence Forces Accountability

Weak cultures avoid accountability.
Competent people demand it.

They:

- ask hard questions
- challenge assumptions
- notice inconsistencies
- speak precisely
- see risks early
- identify flaws in reasoning
- expect follow-through

This pressure makes others uncomfortable.

Not because the competent person is wrong,
but because they are often right.

Competence Cuts Through Politics

In political environments, status is earned through relationships — not performance.

Competence disrupts this system because it:

- bypasses hierarchy
- accelerates execution
- generates influence
- builds credibility
- reduces dependency on approval

- exposes unnecessary roles

Competence makes politics less effective.

Political people do not appreciate this.

Competence Feels Unfair to the Insecure

People who struggle often believe they are trying their hardest. To them, the success of competent individuals feels like:

- luck
- favoritism
- extra support
- better circumstances
- someone having it "easier"

Rarely do they interpret competence as skill earned through effort.

Because acknowledging competence would require acknowledging their own shortcomings.

Ego resists that.

Competence Is Hard to Manipulate

In weak cultures, people gain leverage by controlling information, process, or relationships.

Competent people disrupt this by:

- understanding systems quickly
- learning fast

- eliminating inefficiencies
- calling out nonsense
- refusing to play the game
- creating clarity
- producing results without politics

This threatens people who rely on compliance and confusion for influence.

The Fear Behind the Threat

When someone says a competent person is "intimidating," what they usually mean is:

- "They see things I miss."
- "They set a standard I can't reach."
- "They ask questions I can't answer."
- "They make me feel insecure."
- "They don't need my approval."
- "They are harder to manipulate."
- "They force me to improve."
- "They show my weaknesses."

Competence feels threatening because it challenges the ego.

The threat is rarely the competent person.
The threat is what they represent.

Competence Is a Cultural Test

In healthy cultures:

- competence is valued
- competence is rewarded
- competence is studied
- competence is shared
- competence lifts everyone

In unhealthy cultures:

- competence is resented
- competence is minimized
- competence is framed as arrogance
- competence is politically punished
- competence is ignored
- competence is isolated

Competence reveals the true culture of any organization.

Not through surveys.

Not through mission statements.

But through how people respond to those who excel.

Competence Needs Protection

Competent people burn out in weak environments because they:

- get overloaded
- become default problem-solvers
- receive more responsibility without authority
- get punished for high standards

- are asked to fix systemic issues
- are blamed when things go wrong
- are under-promoted and over-utilized

Organizations often exploit competence instead of elevating it.

When competence threatens the wrong people,
leaders must protect competence —
or it will disappear.

Competence Is Not the Threat — Ego Is

The real threat is not the capable individual.
It is the fragile ego that cannot tolerate comparison.

The ego prefers equality of outcome over equality of effort.
It prefers comfort over growth.
It prefers politics over merit.
It prefers illusion over truth.

Competence is threatening because it cuts through all illusions.

It reveals reality.
It clarifies truth.
It elevates standards.
It demands accountability.
It tests humility.
It seeks continual improvement.

Competence doesn't make people uncomfortable.
Ego does.

The Hard Truth

Competence is not offensive.
Competence is not arrogant.
Competence is not aggressive.

Competence is simply **clear**.

It is clarity of thought, action, judgment, responsibility, and results.

And clarity is uncomfortable for people who hide behind process and confusion.

Competence threatens only those who fear exposure.

For everyone else, competence is oxygen.

It is hope.
It is progress.
It is the foundation for continual improvement and excellence.

Because at the end of the day:

Competence isn't a threat.
It's the solution.

Chapter 16
Why People Prefer Certainty Over Truth

Human beings say they want truth.

They claim to value:
- honesty
- transparency
- objectivity
- open discussion
- rational thinking

But in practice, people prefer **certainty** — even when that certainty is false.

Certainty feels safe.
Truth feels dangerous.

Certainty comforts the ego.
Truth confronts it.

Certainty creates stability.
Truth creates disruption.

This is why people will cling to a confident lie over an uncomfortable truth.

And why organizations, cultures, and even families build entire belief systems around what feels certain, rather than what is accurate.

The preference for certainty is everywhere —
and it is one of the main reasons systems break.

Truth Is Complex. Certainty Is Simple.

Truth is rarely straightforward.

Truth is nuanced.

Truth is conditional.

Truth requires context.

Truth changes with new information.

Truth often contains contradiction.

Truth forces uncomfortable questions.

Certainty, on the other hand, is simple.

- "This is the right way."
- "That is the wrong way."
- "We've always done it like this."
- "That's the process."
- "Leadership decided."

Certainty removes the burden of thinking.
It removes the discomfort of ambiguity.
It removes the fear of responsibility.

Truth demands effort.
Certainty demands obedience.

Why People Crave Certainty

There are three psychological drivers behind the desire for certainty:

1. Fear of the unknown

Humans evolved to avoid uncertainty — because uncertainty used to mean danger.
In the modern world, uncertainty means possibility.
But the brain doesn't easily distinguish the two.

2. Fear of being wrong

Truth forces people to evaluate their own assumptions.
Certainty allows people to feel secure, even if that security is imaginary.

3. Fear of loss of control

Uncertainty makes people feel powerless.
Certainty gives the illusion of control.

The keyword is **illusion** — but for most people, illusion is enough.

Certainty Is an Emotional Comfort, Not an Intellectual Position

Most certainty is emotional in origin and makes sense only in hindsight.

People decide what feels safe, then rationalize it later.

This is why:
- people defend broken processes
- leaders cling to bad strategies
- teams resist new ideas
- organizations avoid uncomfortable truths
- families maintain dysfunctional patterns

Certainty feels like stability.
Truth feels like risk.

The Illusion of Stability

Certainty is attractive because it creates the impression that:
- things make sense
- problems are solvable
- leadership knows what it's doing
- the future is predictable
- complexity is controllable

This illusion is extremely powerful, especially in large organizations.

People would rather operate under a flawed but clear assumption than deal with the anxiety of not knowing.

That's why bad policies last far longer than good ones.

How Certainty Breaks Organizations

Organizations built on certainty instead of truth exhibit predictable failures:

1. They punish dissent

Anyone who introduces uncertainty becomes a threat.

Not because they're wrong,
but because they disrupt emotional comfort.

2. They cling to outdated assumptions

Certainty replaces thinking.

The world changes.
The organization doesn't.

3. They value confidence over competence

People who speak boldly win.
People who think carefully lose.

This creates a dangerous leadership structure.

4. They make decisions to preserve narrative, not reality

Admitting the truth would require admitting mistakes.
Certainty ensures no admission is ever required.

5. They fall behind more adaptive competitors

Flexible systems evolve.

Rigid systems die.

Certainty creates rigidity.

Certainty Loves Absolutes

Truth lives in complexity.

Certainty lives in absolutes.

Certainty thrives on:
- binary thinking
- simple narratives
- easy villains
- clear heroes
- rigid roles
- "us vs. them" frameworks

It reduces the world to digestible pieces —
even if those pieces are fiction.

This is why certainty is a powerful political tool and a terrible management tool.

Truth Requires Maturity

Truth demands qualities many people struggle to develop:
- humility
- patience

- curiosity
- tolerance for discomfort
- intellectual flexibility
- emotional regulation
- willingness to revise beliefs
- openness to challenge
- acceptance of ambiguity
- continually evolving

These traits are often mistaken for weakness.
They are actually signs of strength.

Certainty feels strong.
Truth requires strength.

Certainty Avoids Accountability

A person operating from certainty says:

- "This is the right answer."
- "This is the correct path."
- "This is how it must be done."

But if the answer is wrong or the path fails,
certainty gives them an escape:

- "It wasn't my fault."
- "That was the policy."
- "That was the process."
- "Everyone agreed."

Certainty isn't just comfortable —

it's convenient.

Truth exposes responsibility.
Certainty hides it.

Organizations Built on Truth Look Different

Healthy, high-performing systems embrace truth, even when it's uncomfortable.

They reward:
- questioning
- analysis
- data
- experimentation
- curiosity
- intellectual honesty
- debate
- iteration
- transparency
- abandoning outdated assumptions

Truth-based organizations are flexible.
They evolve.
They survive change.

Certainty-based organizations resist change —
until they collapse under it.

The Competence Connection

Competent people gravitate toward truth.

Incompetent people gravitate toward certainty.

Because:
- competence thrives in reality
- ego thrives in simplicity
- skill requires adaptation
- insecurity requires fixed narratives

Competence is comfortable with nuance.
Incompetence demands simplicity.

That is why competent people often become cultural threats in weak organizations —
they introduce truth where people want certainty.

The Hard Truth

Human beings do not naturally seek truth.
They seek safety.

Certainty provides that safety, even when it is false.
Truth removes that safety, even when it is necessary.

But truth has something certainty does not:

truth compounds.

Over time:
- truth strengthens systems

- truth improves decisions
- truth reveals opportunity
- truth prevents disasters
- truth accelerates progress

Certainty only delays reality.

And delayed reality always returns with interest.

The organizations, leaders, and individuals who succeed long-term are the ones who choose truth — even when it's uncomfortable, inconvenient, or disruptive.

Because while certainty may feel good today…
truth is what survives tomorrow.

Chapter 17
Why People Avoid Responsibility

Responsibility is admired in theory and avoided in practice.

Everyone claims to value responsibility:

- "We need accountable leaders."
- "We want people who take ownership."
- "We reward initiative."

But when responsibility shows up in its real form —
when it demands decision, action, risk, and consequences —
people scatter.

Not because they are lazy.
Not because they are malicious.
But because responsibility requires three things most people struggle with:

1. **Courage**
2. **Exposure**
3. **Discomfort**

Responsibility is heavy.

Most people would rather carry something lighter — like opinions.

Responsibility Comes with Weight

Responsibility is not a title.
It is not a job description.
It is not a task list.

Responsibility is **the willingness to accept the responsibility if something fails.**

This weight comes with:
- scrutiny
- consequences
- accountability
- visibility
- expectations
- ownership
- pressure

Most people don't dislike responsibility because they fear failure.
They dislike the emotional burden that comes with it.

Why People Fear Responsibility

The avoidance of responsibility is rooted in four psychological fears:

1. Fear of blame

If you own the work,

you own the mistakes.
Most people want credit without exposure.

2. Fear of failure

Responsibility removes the ability to hide.
Failure becomes personal, not collective.

3. Fear of judgment

Taking responsibility exposes your competence —
or the lack of it.

People would rather look vague than look wrong.

4. Fear of losing control

Responsibility demands action in uncertain conditions.
People want guarantees before they act.
Responsibility does not provide guarantees.

These fears are universal.
Avoidance is the instinctive response.

The Comfort of Shared Responsibility

Shared responsibility feels safe.

"If we all own it, no one can be singled out."

This sounds cooperative.
It is actually protective.

Shared responsibility is the most elegant way to ensure:
- no accountability
- no ownership
- no clarity
- no consequences
- no progress

It is a socially acceptable avoidance strategy.

Nothing dies faster than a task owned by a committee.

Responsibility Requires Maturity

Responsibility demands traits many adults never develop:
- emotional regulation
- calm under pressure
- humility
- self-honesty
- long-term thinking
- independence
- decisiveness
- resilience

These traits do not come from age.

They come from experience, hardship, and repeated exposure to real consequences.

Responsibility is a maturity test.
Many people fail it quietly.

Most Systems Punish Responsibility

Even worse:

Many organizations claim to value ownership but structurally punish it.

Here's how:

1. Blame culture

Mistakes are weaponized.
People learn: "Don't step forward."

2. Micromanagement

Taking initiative invites interference.

3. Lack of authority

People are asked to own outcomes without empowerment.

4. Political environments

Credit is stolen.
Blame is redistributed downward, success is taken by seniors.

5. No clear decision-making structure

Responsibility becomes dangerous in ambiguity.

6. Leaders who avoid responsibility themselves

When leaders deflect responsibility, everyone else follows.

People avoid responsibility for rational reasons —
because the system teaches them to avoid it.

The Illusion of Responsibility

Many people perform responsibility instead of practicing it.

They use phrases like:
- "I'm on it."
- "Let me circle back."
- "I'll take this offline."
- "We're coordinating."
- "I'll provide visibility."

These are not signs of responsibility.
They are signs of activity.

Real responsibility shows up in results, not rhetoric.

Responsibility Requires Saying 'I' Instead of 'We'

False responsibility hides behind the word "we."
- "We need to do better."
- "We should align on this."
- "We dropped the ball."
- "We need a better plan."

Real responsibility uses the word **I**:
- "I missed this."

- "I will fix it."
- "I own the outcome."
- "I made the call."
- "I take responsibility."

Most people avoid the word "I" because it removes the safety of diffusion and puts a risky outcome directly on them.

Why High Performers Take Responsibility Easily

High performers don't fear responsibility — they embrace it.

Why?

Because they understand five truths:

1. Responsibility creates influence

Influence follows ownership.
People trust those who take responsibility voluntarily.

2. Responsibility accelerates learning

Nothing teaches faster than being accountable for outcomes.

3. Responsibility creates clarity

When you own the work, ambiguity disappears.

4. Responsibility builds confidence

Courage grows only through exposure.

5. Responsibility drives career growth

Organizations may favor politics in the short term,
but they favor ownership in the long term.

Responsibility is leverage.
Avoidance is stagnation.

Why Low Performers Fear Responsibility

Low performers tend to avoid responsibility because it removes their primary defense mechanisms:

- hiding in the group
- blending into the workflow
- blaming circumstances
- shifting expectation
- relying on ambiguity
- deflecting accountability

Responsibility shines a spotlight.
Some people do not want to be seen.

Responsibility Is a Cultural Indicator

You can diagnose any organization by asking one question:

"Who takes responsibility when something goes wrong?"

The answer reveals everything:
- If everyone blames the system → weak culture
- If people blame others → political culture
- If leaders blame employees → toxic culture
- If silence follows → fearful culture
- If someone steps forward → strong culture
- If multiple people step forward → exceptional culture

Responsibility is the clearest window into organizational health.

Why Responsibility Is Rare

Responsibility requires five things most environments do not provide:
- **clear expectations**
- **psychological safety**
- **empowered decision-making**
- **balanced accountability**
- **leaders who model the behavior**

Without these elements, responsibility becomes risky.

When responsibility is punished, people retreat.

When responsibility is rewarded, people rise.

The Hard Truth

People do not avoid responsibility because they are weak.
They avoid it because responsibility is expensive.

Responsibility costs:
- comfort
- safety
- ego
- excuses
- emotional protection

But responsibility also provides the only thing that truly matters:

power.

Not authority.
Not title.
Not appearance.

Power — the ability to create change, influence outcomes, and shape the world around you.

Responsibility may be heavy,
but it is the weight that builds strength.

And the individuals — and organizations — who embrace responsibility are the ones who rise.

Chapter 18
Why People Avoid Thinking

People love to *feel* like they are thinking.

They love:
- discussing
- debating
- analyzing
- brainstorming
- planning
- "whiteboarding"
- collecting opinions
- forming committees

But none of those activities require real thinking.

Real thinking is rare.
Real thinking is hard.
Real thinking is uncomfortable.

Most people will do almost anything to avoid it.

Not because they're incapable,

but because **real thinking requires effort, honesty, and courage** — three things the human ego naturally resists.

The Illusion of Thought

Most thinking is not thinking.

It is:

- reacting
- remembering
- repeating
- rationalizing
- defending
- pattern matching
- defaulting to habit
- seeking confirmation

This feels like thinking because it produces mental activity. But activity is not depth.

Thinking isn't about *having thoughts.*
Thinking is about **evaluating them.**

Most people never evaluate their thoughts.
They simply obey them.

Why Real Thinking Is So Difficult

Thinking — real thinking — requires facing things people try desperately to avoid.

1. Thinking requires confronting uncertainty.

Humans dislike uncertainty.
We evolved to replace uncertainty with instinct.

Thinking demands:
- doubt
- analysis
- reconsideration
- questioning
- humility

This is psychologically uncomfortable.

2. Thinking requires being wrong.

To think well, you must accept the possibility that:
- your assumptions are flawed
- your beliefs are outdated
- your understanding is incomplete
- your perspective is limited

Most people would rather defend a bad idea
than admit they need a new one.

3. Thinking requires responsibility.

Once you understand something clearly, you are responsible for acting on it.

This is why ignorance feels so comfortable.
Ignorance protects people from accountability.

4. Thinking requires mental energy.

The brain is designed to conserve energy.
Thinking burns calories.

This is why people default to:

- shortcuts
- habits
- routines
- scripts
- clichés
- opinions
- group consensus

It saves effort — even if it costs clarity.

People Prefer Feeling Right Over Being Right

Real thinking often reveals that:

- you were wrong
- your assumption was false
- your earlier judgment was emotional
- the situation is more complex than you hoped

Feeling right creates certainty.
Thinking disrupts certainty.

Most people choose the comfort of feeling right.

This is why opinions are more common than insight.

Thinking Requires Slowness — The Modern World Rewards Speed

Real thinking is slow.

It demands time to:

- observe
- reflect
- integrate information
- evaluate options
- challenge assumptions
- connect ideas
- abstract patterns

But modern environments reward the opposite:

- speed
- immediacy
- constant response
- real-time feedback
- instant opinions
- instant reactions

People no longer pause long enough to think.
They react, then justify the reaction later.

Thinking Requires Emotional Distance

People cannot think clearly when they are:

- anxious

- angry
- defensive
- fearful
- insecure
- overwhelmed

Thinking requires calm.
Calm requires space.
Space requires boundaries.

Most environments — and most people — offer none.

Thinking Requires Intellectual Honesty

Most people use their intelligence not to discover truth, but to defend themselves from it.

They use intellect to:
- justify
- explain
- rationalize
- defend
- protect their identity

Real thinking requires honesty so deep it feels almost surgical.

You must be willing to say:
- "I was wrong."
- "I don't know."
- "I need to revise this."
- "My initial belief was emotional, not logical."

- "I'm making excuses."

Most people cannot do this without ego collapse.

Why Organizations Avoid Thinking

Organizations avoid thinking for the same reasons individuals do:

1. Thinking threatens authority

Real thinking questions decisions.
Systems that rely on hierarchy resist questioning.

2. Thinking reveals inefficiency

If people truly thought through the processes they follow,
half of them would be eliminated tomorrow.

3. Thinking slows things down

Leaders often want speed more than clarity.
Thinking demands the opposite.

4. Thinking exposes incompetence

Not everyone in leadership wants to be evaluated on truth.
Certainty protects position.

5. Thinking leads to change

And change threatens comfort.

Organizations say they want innovation —

but innovation requires thinking, and thinking requires disruption.

So most organizations end up innovating only in PowerPoint.

The Substitutes People Use Instead of Thinking

People use many activities to simulate thinking:
- endless meetings
- repeated discussions
- status updates
- brainstorming sessions
- consensus building
- spreadsheet tweaking
- risk-avoidance analysis
- writing long emails
- planning instead of doing
- talking instead of deciding

These activities create the *appearance* of thought without the benefits of it.

Real thinking leads to decision.
Simulated thinking leads to activity.

Thinking Requires Isolation — People Fear Being Alone with Their Mind

To think deeply, you must be willing to be alone.

- alone with uncertainty
- alone with responsibility
- alone with your own limitations
- alone with difficult questions

Most people avoid this solitude through:

- noise
- distraction
- social validation
- constant motion
- digital stimulation

You cannot think deeply while trying to avoid your own thoughts.

Thinking Is a Competitive Advantage

Because so few people think — really think —
the ability to do so becomes an enormous advantage.

People who think clearly:

- solve problems faster
- make better decisions
- reduce complexity
- avoid drama
- bypass politics

- gain influence
- earn trust
- rise quickly
- see patterns others miss

Thinking is leverage.
Lack of thinking is stagnation.

Thinking Creates Courage

Thinking brings clarity.
Clarity creates confidence.
Confidence creates action.

Avoiding thought leaves people:
- fearful
- uncertain
- reactive
- defensive
- dependent on others

Thinking is the foundation of courage.

The Hard Truth

Most people are not afraid of thinking.
They are afraid of what thinking will reveal.

Because thinking reveals:
- truth

- responsibility
- consequences
- personal limitations
- uncomfortable realities

It dismantles illusions one by one —
and illusions are what people use to stay emotionally safe. Illusions are reinforced in groups and social media.

But illusions don't build strong people.
They build fragile ones.

Thinking is the path to strength.
Strength is the path to freedom.

And the individuals — and organizations — willing to actually think are the ones who shape the future.

Chapter 19
Why People Avoid Decisions

Decision-making should be simple.

You evaluate the options, pick one, and move forward like a functioning adult.

But people don't do that.

People treat decisions like unexploded ordnance: dangerous, unpredictable, and best handled by someone else.

If you've ever watched a group of professionals attempt to choose a lunch location, you've seen the human condition in its rawest form.

Everyone suddenly becomes a philosopher, weighing existential trade-offs between tacos and sandwiches as if the fate of civilization hangs in the balance.

People Don't Avoid Decisions Because They're Hard — They Avoid Them Because They're Real

A decision is a line in the sand.

It forces commitment, and commitment forces accountability, and accountability forces the horrifying realization that *you* might be the one responsible if things go wrong.

And people love responsibility until the moment it becomes real.
Then they love "collaboration," "alignment," and "more information."

Translation:
"I don't want to choose, but I'd love to be involved in not choosing."

The Four Reasons People Avoid Decisions

People avoid decisions for the same four reasons they avoid cleaning their garage:

1. **There might be something unpleasant in there.**
   Mistakes. Expectations. A dead pigeon of regret. Who knows?

2. **They think they'll do it later.**
   Spoiler: they won't.

3. **They're waiting for 'the right time.'**
   The right time never arrives.
   It's like waiting for a Tuesday that feels like a Friday.

4. **Someone else might do it for them.**
   Hope is not a strategy, but for many, it's the preferred one.

People Love Options More Than Outcomes

People overvalue optionality.
They cling to choices like dragons guarding treasure.

"Let's not commit yet," they say.
"We should keep our options open."

Keeping options open feels smart.
It feels strategic.
It feels like maintaining control.

But it also prevents progress, momentum, clarity, and results — the four things people say they want while actively sabotaging them.

The Safety Blanket of Endless Input

When someone doesn't want to decide, they put on a performance called **Seeking Input.**

Seeking Input is the adult version of asking your friends if you should text your ex.

- "What do you think?"
- "What do others think?"
- "What does the data say?"
- "What does the other data say?"
- "What does the data about the data say?"

At some point, "gathering information" transitions into "stalling because I'm afraid to choose."

But no one admits that.
They frame it as being thorough.

Meetings: Where Decisions Go to Die

If you really want to avoid a decision, schedule a meeting.

Better yet, schedule a recurring meeting.

Meetings are the padded rooms where decisions are gently suffocated under layers of:

- Updates
- Roundtable opinions
- "Just to circle back"
- "Let's take this offline"
- "We're really close"
- "Let's table this"

By the time the meeting ends, no one remembers the original question — which IS the point.

The Myth of Needing More Information

People tell themselves they need more information to decide.

They don't.

Most decisions only require:

- basic context
- approximate direction
- and a pulse

But people demand certainty, even when the situation itself is inherently uncertain.

It's like refusing to leave the driveway until all traffic lights in the city are green.

Indecision Is Disguised as Intelligence

People who overthink look thoughtful.
People who hesitate look cautious.
People who can't choose look "strategic."

Indecision has incredible PR.

It's marketed as:

- "due diligence"
- "careful analysis"
- "risk management"
- "collaboration"

But indecision is not intelligence.
It's just fear in a suit.

When No One Decides, Everyone Suffers

A group without decisions is a group without direction.
Everyone is working, but no one is moving.

You get:

- stalled projects
- confused teams
- frustrated high-performers
- empowered low-performers

- leaders in name only
- chaos wrapped in a calendar invite

Indecision is not neutral.
It is corrosive.

Why High Performers Decide Faster

High performers understand a simple truth:

You cannot steer a parked car.

A decision — even an imperfect one — creates movement.
Movement creates information.
Information creates clarity.
Clarity creates improvement.

Low performers wait for clarity before moving.
High performers move to create clarity.

One of these groups rises.
The other forms committees.

The Hard Truth

Most people don't avoid decisions because the decision is hard.
They avoid decisions because **making one means they can no longer hide behind ambiguity.**

Once you pick a direction, you can be judged.
Once you choose, you can be wrong.
Once you act, you can fail.

People avoid decisions because decisions make them visible.

But the only thing more dangerous than making the wrong decision is making no decision at all.

Movement beats safety.
Progress beats perfection.
Decisions beat excuses.

Leaders choose.
Everyone else waits.

Chapter 20
Why People Misjudge Risk

Humans are terrible at evaluating risk.

This shouldn't surprise anyone.

These are the same creatures who regularly microwave metal, trust expiration dates "as a suggestion," buy extended warranties on toaster ovens and whose losses pay for hundreds of luxurious casinos.

If there were a global ranking of species by decision-making ability, humans may be slightly above squirrels.

Risk evaluation is just not our thing.

People Fear the Wrong Things

People are terrified of unlikely disasters:
- plane crashes
- shark attacks
- lightning strikes
- poisoned Halloween candy
- the wrong color Gatorade

Meanwhile, they show zero concern for things that actually ruin lives:
- poor financial habits
- staying in bad jobs
- ignoring health
- hiring toxic people
- refusing to learn skills
- never making a decision at all

Humans are emotionally allergic to realistic risks but fully committed to imaginary ones.

Risk Isn't About Probability — It's About Emotion

Risk should be simple:

"What are the chances this will go wrong, and how bad will it be if it does?"

But that's not how people think.

People decide based on:
- feelings
- gut instincts
- childhood memories
- random anecdotes
- what their cousin posted on Facebook
- whatever catastrophe the news mentioned last week

People don't evaluate risk — they **feel** risk.

And feelings are notoriously bad at math.

People Overestimate Dramatic Risks

If something is scary, vivid, or cinematic, the brain assumes it's common.

People think skydiving is risky.
It isn't.
They think rollercoasters are risky.
They aren't.
They think public speaking will kill them.
It won't, unless the audience is armed.

Now compare that to the things people ignore:
- debt
- inactivity
- bad diet
- long-term stress
- mediocre habits
- choosing "safe" but miserable career paths

These things quietly destroy people.
But because they aren't dramatic, people don't take them seriously.

People Underestimate Slow Risks

Slow risks feel harmless because nothing immediately explodes.
- Eating poorly?
  "It's just a snack."

- Skipping goals for another year?
  "I'll start when life calms down."

- Staying in the same job for ten years?
  "At least it's stable."

Slow risks are the most dangerous because the consequences arrive slowly, silently, and inevitably.

If drowning took five years, people would ignore that too.

Risk by Committee: The Worst Form of Risk Assessment

If you put five people in a room and ask them to evaluate risk, you won't get clarity.

You'll get:
- fears
- personal preferences
- worst-case storytelling
- projections of insecurity
- someone Googling stats out of context
- another person insisting "we should be cautious"
- a third saying "let's not overthink this" while absolutely overthinking it

The meeting will end with the same conclusion every committee reaches:

"Let's gather more information."

Or perhaps worse, "Let's take this isolated action which we **could** agree on which we determined when went down the rabbit hole"

...sine Alice in Wonderland is where we should learn risk management.

Committees don't reduce risk.
They distribute anxiety across more people.

Bad At Risk? Great — Let's Make It a Job Requirement

Most corporate cultures train people to misjudge risk by rewarding the appearance of caution over the practice of judgment.

In many workplaces:

- taking action is "risky"
- making decisions is "risky"
- owning your work is "risky"
- moving quickly is "risky"
- trying something new is "risky"

But doing nothing?
Waiting?
Stalling?
Redirecting?
Escalating?
Asking for one more review?

Those are considered "careful."

Organizations aren't risk-averse.

They're *accountability-averse*.

People Think Risk Is About Safety — It's Actually About Trade-Offs

Risk isn't about avoiding danger.
It's about choosing which danger you prefer.

Every option contains risk:

- Staying safe = risk of stagnation
- Taking action = risk of mistakes
- Staying in comfort = risk of regret
- Moving forward = risk of discomfort
- Waiting forever = risk of losing everything

The real question is not whether there is risk,
but **which risk leads somewhere worth going.**

High Performers See Risk Differently

High performers don't avoid risk — they evaluate it.

They ask questions normal people don't:

- "What if this works?"
- "What if the downside isn't that big?"
- "What's the risk of doing nothing?"
- "What information actually matters?"
- "What's the smallest/simplest step I can take to test this?"

They understand that most risks are manageable,

and the real danger is indecision.

High performers treat risk like a steering wheel.
Everyone else treats it like a bomb.

Why Most People Stay Stuck

Bad risk judgment keeps people exactly where they are:

- afraid to start
- afraid to try
- afraid to change
- afraid to ask
- afraid to commit
- afraid to decide

So they stay in the safest place they know:
the same place they were last year.

Most people aren't trapped.
They're anchored.

And the anchor is misjudged risk.

The Hard Truth

Risk isn't the problem.
Your relationship with risk is the problem.

People avoid "risky" things that would improve their lives
and cling to "safe" choices that quietly destroy them.

If you want to grow,
you have to stop treating risk like danger
and start treating it like oxygen.

The goal isn't to eliminate risk.
It's to choose risks worth taking.

Chapter 21
Why Organizations Resist Simplicity

If there's one thing organizations hate, it's simplicity.

Simple ideas? Suspicious.

Simple solutions? Probably wrong.

Simple processes? "We should add a workflow."

Simple decisions? "Let's get more data."

Simplicity threatens everything organizations hold sacred: meetings, committees, dashboards, diagrams, and the illusion of progress.

If a problem ever gets solved too quickly, someone will feel robbed of the opportunity to give a 37-slide presentation about it.

Why Complexity Feels Safer Than Simplicity

People like complexity because it creates the appearance of intelligence.

If you say,

"We need a multi-phase cross-functional operational alignment initiative,"
you sound smart and expand your reporting chain.

If you say,
"Let's stop doing dumb things,"
you sound reckless.

Complexity hides incompetence.
Simplicity exposes it.

Complexity Gives People a Place to Hide

Simplicity is dangerous because it shines a light directly on the real problem.

And the real problem is often:
- broken processes
- unclear ownership
- bad management
- weak leadership
- political nonsense
- unnecessary work
- lack of accountability

Complexity gives everyone camouflage.

The more complicated the system,
the harder it is to notice who's not doing anything.

The Simple Solution Test (Organizations Fail It Every Time)

When presented with a simple solution, most organizations respond the same way:

1. **Panic**
   "That feels too easy."

2. **Suspicion**
   "What are we missing?"

3. **Scope Creep**
   "Let's add another team to review it."

4. **Translation**
   "We need a new acronym."

5. **Death by Meeting**
   "Let's schedule a planning session."

Simple solutions don't stick in organizations because organizations need complexity to justify their existence.

The Myth That 'Complex Problems Require Complex Solutions'

This sounds wise.
It's actually an excuse.

Most complex problems come from **simple failures**:

- unclear goals

- bad incentives
- poor communication
- no ownership
- lack of standards

But complex systems make people feel important,
so they multiply complexity instead of subtracting it.

It's easier to build a maze than to close the door.

Why Leaders Fear Simplicity

Simplicity requires:

- clarity
- commitment
- decisiveness
- accountability

Leaders avoid simplicity because it removes the ability to hide behind:

- jargon
- ambiguity
- theoretical complexity
- strategic fog
- "We need to think more about this"

Simplicity demands that a leader actually lead,
which is inconvenient for leaders who prefer appearances.

Complexity Creates Jobs — Not Results

One of the unspoken truths of organizational life is:

Complexity keeps people employed.

Every new:

- process
- workflow
- review cycle
- dashboard
- communication channel
- compliance document
- cross-functional initiative

...creates more work for someone.

Simplicity threatens this ecosystem of unnecessary employment.

This is why bureaucracy grows forever
and results stay exactly the same.

Why High Performers Gravitate Toward Simplicity

High performers like simplicity because:

- it makes decisions easier
- it speeds up execution
- it highlights real problems
- it removes noise
- it clarifies ownership

- it exposes nonsense
- it makes accountability unavoidable

Simplicity is a spotlight.

High performers aren't afraid to stand in it.

Low performers prefer shadows.

The Organizational Life Cycle of Complexity

Every organization eventually follows this path:

1. **Start simple** — because there's no time for anything else.
2. **Grow** — and add a little structure.
3. **Add more structure** — because someone read a book.
4. **Add more process** — because someone messed up once.
5. **Add meetings** — because no one knows what's happening anymore.
6. **Add committees** — to discuss why nothing is happening.
7. **Become paralyzed** — but look very professional doing it.

Complexity is not the result of growth.

It is the result of avoiding hard conversations.

Simplicity Requires Courage

Creating simplicity means deciding what matters.

Deciding what matters means saying no.

Saying no means upsetting people.

That's why organizations resist simplicity:

D.M. Christensen

simplicity forces choices,
and choices create conflict.

People say they want clarity
until clarity holds them accountable.

The Hard Truth

Complexity is comforting.
Simplicity is confronting.

Organizations choose the comfort of complexity
over the discomfort of clarity
every single time.

If you want progress,
start removing —
not adding.

Because the simplest systems run faster,
the simplest structures produce results,
and the simplest decisions move people forward.

Everything else is just decoration.

Chapter 22
Why Complexity Gets Confused with Intelligence

There is no greater magic trick in modern professional life than looking smart by making something unnecessarily complicated.

You've seen it.

Someone explains a simple process like they're revealing the Dead Sea Scrolls, complete with arrows, acronyms, diagrams, and words that don't need to exist.

Suddenly, ordering office supplies involves a "Cross-Functional Vertical Procurement Enablement Funnel."

This isn't intelligence.
This is performance art.

The Performance of Looking Smart

People love to *sound* intelligent more than they like to *be* intelligent.

This is why they use sentences like:
- "We need to operationalize the cross-domain workflow."
- "We're leveraging a multi-dimensional alignment strategy."
- "Our solution integrates synergistic paradigm frameworks."

Translation:

"We are saying nothing, but saying it loudly."

Complexity is the costume.
Intelligence is the actor.
And most people are wearing the costume with no actor inside.

Why People Choose Complicated Over Clear

There are a few very human reasons:

1. Complicated = Impressive

If you say something in a simple way, people think anyone could have said it.
If you say something in a confusing way, people assume you're a genius.

It's the same logic that makes people buy wine they can't pronounce.

2. Complicated = Safe

The more tangled your explanation,
the harder it is for anyone to challenge you.

You can't be wrong if no one knows what you just said.

3. Complicated = Job Security

If your job can be explained in two sentences,
someone might realize they can replace you.

If it takes three diagrams and a glossary,
you're safe.

And probably overpaid.

The Greatest Misconception in Professional Life

People genuinely believe that *complex ideas require complex explanations.*

Wrong.

If you understand something well,
you can explain it to a 12-year-old.

If you don't,
you'll create a PowerPoint with 48 layers.

This is why the smartest people talk plainly,
and the least competent people talk like malfunctioning corporate robots.

D.M. Christensen

The Real Work Happens After the Complicated People Leave

You've seen this too:

A meeting ends.

The jargon evaporates.

The adults in the room sigh loudly.

Then someone says,
"Okay… what are we actually doing?"

That's when actual intelligence begins.
Quietly.
Calmly.
Without buzzwords.

Real intelligence solves.
Simulated intelligence performs.

Complexity Is Often a Cover-Up

When someone refuses to explain something simply, it's usually because of one of three reasons:

1. They don't understand it themselves.
2. They don't want to be questioned.
3. They want to look important.

All three are incompetence wearing a suit.

Why Simplicity Threatens People

Simplicity demands:

- clear thinking
- real decisions
- fewer excuses
- fewer hiding places
- fewer people pretending to work

This is terrifying for people who rely on:

- ambiguity
- confusion
- "alignment sessions"
- interpretive dance–style project plans

Simplicity always exposes two types of people:

1. Those who get things done.
2. Those who pretend to get things done.

And guess which group fights simplicity the hardest?

How Organizations Trick Themselves

Companies love complexity because it feels sophisticated.

They build:

- complex strategies
- complex job titles
- complex approval flows
- complex compensation systems

- complex dashboards
- complex org charts shaped like DNA strands

Then wonder why nothing moves.

A simple plan is scary because it removes excuses.
A complex plan is comforting because it ensures nothing is ever really your fault.

High Performers Speak Clearly

Truly competent people have no need for theatrics.

They say things like:
- "This is broken."
- "Here's how we fix it."
- "I'll take responsibility."
- "This is the real problem."
- "We don't need twelve steps. We need two."

This clarity is often mistaken for oversimplification.

It's not oversimplification.
It's understanding.

The Hard Truth

Complexity is a smokescreen.
Clarity is a spotlight.

One hides the truth.

The other exposes it.

Most people choose the smokescreen.
High performers choose the spotlight.

Because anyone can make something complicated.
It takes actual intelligence to make it simple.

Chapter 23
Why Most People Plateau

Most people don't fail.
They just... stop.

Not dramatically.
Not with fireworks.
Not even with a meltdown spectacular enough to post on TikTok.

They simply reach a point where they decide—subconsciously, quietly, and with absolutely no self-awareness—that they have grown "enough."

And then they spend the next 30 years wondering why nothing feels exciting anymore.

The plateau is life's most comfortable prison.
And most people are serving a life sentence.

The Plateau Isn't a Cliff. It's a Couch.

People imagine plateauing as falling off a professional cliff.

It's not.

It's sinking into a soft, warm, emotionally comforting couch and saying: "This is fine. I could stay here forever."

And then they do.

They trade growth for comfort, identity for familiarity, and potential for predictability—because predictability is easier on the ego.

Unfortunately for them, the business world never stays the same

Why People Plateau (The Real Reasons They Never Admit)

People don't plateau because they're incapable.
They plateau because growth asks questions they don't want to answer.

1. Plateauing protects the ego.

To grow, you must admit you need to grow.

This requires:
- being wrong
- being a beginner
- being awkward
- being slow
- being uncertain
- being imperfect

Most adults would rather fake confidence forever than feel like a novice for one week.

2. Plateauing protects identity.

People cling to roles they've outgrown because those roles feel safe.

"I'm the expert."
"I'm the reliable one."
"I'm the high performer."
"I'm the smartest one here."

Titles become emotional furniture.
Nobody wants to redecorate themselves.

3. Plateauing feels like stability.

People confuse "nothing is happening" with "everything is fine."

If nothing is moving, shifting, breaking, or challenging them, they assume they're succeeding.

Really, they're stagnating.
(Those are different things.)

Success Is the Most Common Cause of Plateauing

People think failure ruins growth.

Wrong.

Success is far more dangerous.

Once someone:

- gets promoted
- feels respected
- earns comfort
- becomes "the go-to person"
- gets competent enough to coast
- stops being questioned

They ease off the gas.

They assume the skill that got them here will carry them forward forever.

But nothing ages faster than competence you stop updating.

The Plateau Always Starts Quietly

People plateau the way glaciers move—slowly, invisibly, and with the illusion of permanence.

Look for the signs:

- They repeat the same solutions.
- They stop asking questions.
- They avoid discomfort.
- They rely on old strengths.
- They protect reputation instead of progress.
- They stop reading, learning, challenging, or experimenting.
- They work *in* their role instead of *beyond* it.
- They talk more than they think.

By the time they notice, the plateau isn't a phase.
It's a personality trait.

Plateauing Is Contagious

Put one stagnant person in a team and suddenly everyone starts lowering their standards so they don't "make others look bad."

This is how mediocrity becomes a team sport.

People adjust to the environment, not the vision.

This is why high performers often leave:
they refuse to be infected.

Why High Performers Don't Plateau

High performers don't avoid plateauing because they're special.
They avoid plateauing because they're allergic to comfort.

They get suspicious when things feel easy.

They get itchy when life feels predictable.

They get uncomfortable when improvement slows.

Most importantly, they reinvent themselves constantly, even when they don't have to.

Especially when they don't have to.

To them, comfort is not a reward—
it's a warning sign.

The Uncomfortable Truth

The reason most people plateau has nothing to do with talent.

It's because growth requires a kind of emotional violence against your own comfort.

You must:
- challenge your identity
- question your assumptions
- break your habits
- expose your weaknesses
- destroy your excuses
- abandon your safety
- outgrow your past self

Most people don't want to grow.
They want to *feel* like they're growing.

So they pick the illusion over the effort.

And then wonder why life never changes.

Our educational system teaches stability, obedience and compliance, not questioning.

The Hard Truth

Plateauing isn't a failure of ability.
It's a failure of honesty.

You don't grow because you don't want to pay the psychological price of growth.

You don't improve because improvement threatens the version of yourself you're comfortable with.

You don't evolve because evolution starts with admitting you haven't evolved.

Comfort is the enemy.
Growth is the rebellion.

And those who choose growth—
choose discomfort, repeatedly, intentionally, forever—
are the only people who become exceptional.

Everyone else becomes predictable.

Chapter 24
The Psychology of Growth

Growth is not inspirational.
It's not pretty.
It's not a sunrise, a mantra, or whatever nonsense they print on yoga mats.

Growth is psychological warfare —
and the person you're fighting is yourself.

No one tells you that.
They tell you to "believe in yourself" and "chase your dreams," as if dreams are hiding under the couch and you just need a flashlight.

But the real enemy is the part of your brain that desperately wants life to stay the same.
The part that hates uncertainty.
The part that panics when you challenge it.
The part that whispers:

"We're comfortable. Why ruin this?"

That voice isn't laziness.

It's survival.
Just the outdated kind.

Growth Hurts Because It Requires an Ego Funeral

Here's the truth no one prints on motivational posters:

To grow, your ego has to die.
Not dramatically — just repeatedly.

Every time you improve, you bury a version of yourself:

- the version that failed to ask questions
- the version that hid behind competence
- the version that hated feedback
- the version that pretended to "already know this stuff"
- the version that flinched at discomfort
- the version that survived on excuses

Growth is a series of small ego funerals.
Some people mourn too much to continue.

Most People Don't Avoid Growth. They Avoid What Growth Reveals.

Growth doesn't expose your potential.
It exposes your limitations.

Which is why people avoid:

- feedback ("my soul has chosen violence today")

- discomfort ("I prefer activities that don't require emotional sweating")
- being wrong ("I read one article on this in 2018 and feel confident that qualifies me")
- uncertainty ("what if this makes me look like I don't know what I'm doing?")

Growth forces you to meet the parts of yourself you've been avoiding for years.

Most adults would rather stay the same than confront the truth about themselves.

The Real Psychology Behind Growth

Growth is an emotional process disguised as a skill-building process.

People don't fail to grow because of:

- lack of opportunity
- lack of intelligence
- lack of time
- lack of resources

People fail to grow because of:

- fragile identity
- fragile ego
- avoidance of responsibility
- fear of looking foolish
- dependence on validation
- addiction to certainty

Growth is not hard.
Admitting you need growth is hard.

Comfort Is the Most Addictive Drug in the World

You can spot someone who hasn't grown in years.
They're incredibly confident — in all the wrong things.

Comfort is seductive because it removes:

- challenge
- risk
- accountability
- self-reflection
- ambition
- hunger

Comfort says:
"You're fine the way you are."

Growth says:
"That's adorable. Now get up."

Comfort wins for most people.

Why High Performers Grow (Even When They Don't Want To)

High performers do not grow because they're fearless.

They grow because fear annoys them.

They hate:
- being stuck
- being predictable
- being average
- being unchallenged
- being stagnant

They have a kind of psychological restlessness that refuses to let them settle.

High performers grow because not growing feels wrong.

To them, comfort isn't relief —
it's a red flag.

Growth Requires Psychological Safety (The Real Kind, Not Corporate Karaoke)

People grow when they feel safe enough to:
- be wrong
- try again
- ask stupid questions
- fail publicly
- challenge themselves
- change their identity
- receive unfiltered feedback

It is not "safe enough to share feelings in a circle while holding a foam stress ball" safe.

Real safety:

"I can screw this up and it won't destroy me."

Without internal safety, growth feels like self-destruction.

Growth Is Slow, Boring, and Absolutely Unavoidable if You Want a Life That Doesn't Suck

Real growth is not dramatic.

It's:

- reading instead of scrolling
- thinking instead of reacting
- asking questions instead of pretending you already know
- choosing discomfort over convenience
- confronting the truth before it becomes a crisis
- learning without needing applause

Growth requires consistency, not hashtags.

It requires humility, not motivation.

It requires self-awareness, not self-affirmation.

The Hard Truth

Most people don't stop growing because they reach their potential.

They stop growing because growth threatens the version of themselves they're emotionally attached to.

Growth requires:
- honesty
- vulnerability
- discomfort
- uncertainty
- courage

If that sounds like a lot...
it is.

That's why so many people plateau forever.

Growth is the rebellion.
Comfort is the sedative.

You choose which one runs your life.

Chapter 25
Why Clarity Is So Rare

Clarity sounds simple.

Everyone says they want it:

- "We need more clarity."
- "Can you clarify that?"
- "Let's get aligned on clarity."
- "We need a clarity session."
  (Which is just a meeting where people read the same slides and walk out even more confused.)

But clarity is rare because clarity is dangerous.

Clarity exposes reality.

Reality exposes competence.

Competence exposes everyone who doesn't have it.

No wonder people avoid clarity like it's a plague.

Confusion Is a Feature, Not a Bug

People pretend confusion is accidental.

It's not.

Confusion is a protective layer — like emotional bubble wrap.

If things are unclear, then:
- You can't be blamed.
- You can't be held responsible.
- You can't be expected to produce anything meaningful.
- You can always say "Well, I didn't know."

Confusion is safety.
Clarity is accountability.

Guess which one people choose?

Why People Hate Clarity (Even While Asking for It)

Clarity forces you to make decisions.
Decisions force responsibility.
Responsibility forces performance.

And performance forces the truth.

Most people don't want the truth.
They want something that *sounds* like the truth but doesn't require any behavioral changes.

Clarity destroys all the comfortable hiding places.

It eliminates:
- ambiguity

- plausible deniability
- "I thought someone else was handling it"
- "We need more information"
- "Let's revisit this next quarter"
- "We're still aligning on next steps"

Clarity says:

"No more excuses. What are you actually doing?"

Most people aren't built for that kind of exposure.

The Real Reason Organizations Avoid Clarity

Clarity makes the incompetent visible.

And modern workplaces are fundamentally allergic to anything that disrupts the fragile political ecosystem where:

- the loudest are rewarded,
- the busiest are praised,
- the confident are promoted,
- the mediocre are protected, and
- the honest are told to "adjust their communication style."

Clarity is a threat to every cushy little fiefdom inside an organization.

Which is why the moment clarity tries to enter the building, someone stops it at the door with,

"Let's take this offline."

Clarity Requires Saying Simple, Uncomfortable Things

Clarity is not complicated.

Clarity is saying the sentences everyone avoids, like:

- "This is your job."
- "No, really, **your** job."
- "This is the deadline."
- "This is the outcome."
- "This is the problem."
- "This isn't working."
- "You need to improve this."
- "We're not doing that anymore."
- "This is what we're actually trying to accomplish."

People act like clarity requires a master's degree.

It does not.

It requires courage.

Most People Don't Want Clarity — They Want Permission

When someone says "I need clarity," they often mean:

- "Tell me what to do so I'm not responsible if it fails."
- "Tell me what you want so I don't have to think."
- "Tell me it's okay to avoid the difficult thing."
- "Tell me my assumptions were correct so my ego stays intact."

Clarity isn't permission.

Clarity is direction.

People get those confused because direction requires initiative, and initiative requires effort.

Effort is exhausting.

High Performers Treat Clarity Like Oxygen

High performers despise ambiguity.

They don't want:
- hints
- vibes
- "soft guidance"
- "general themes"
- "broad strategic intent"
- "a sense of where we're headed"

They want to know:
- What is the actual goal?
- What problem are we solving?
- What needs to happen?
- Who is responsible?
- What does success look like?
- When is it due?
- And why is everyone else so comfortable being confused?

To high performers, clarity isn't pressure.

It's freedom.

When things are clear, they can move.
And when they can move, they can win.

Clarity Isn't a Meeting, a Document, or a Presentation

Clarity is a choice.

A choice to:
- say the real thing
- admit the real problem
- confront the real barriers
- define the real responsibilities
- own the real outcomes

This is why clarity is scarce:

Most people want **harmony** more than truth.
Comfort more than direction.
Agreement more than accountability.

Clarity disrupts all three.

Clarity Has a Cost — But Confusion Has a Bigger One

The cost of clarity:
- discomfort
- honesty
- accountability

- ego bruising
- some awkward conversations

The cost of confusion:

- wasted time
- chaos
- drift
- resentment
- burnout
- finger-pointing
- mediocrity

One is painful.
The other is catastrophic.

The Hard Truth

Clarity is not complicated.
It is not a skill only executives possess or gurus sell.

Clarity is simply the courage to say what everyone already knows but refuses to acknowledge.

That's why clarity is rare:
It requires honesty.
It requires ownership.
It requires responsibility.
It requires a backbone.

And that eliminates most of the population.

The people who embrace clarity rise.

The people who avoid it plateau.

And the people who fear it create the chaos the rest of us have to clean up.

Chapter 26
Why Systems Matter More Than People Think

Everyone loves to talk about "great people."

"We need great people."

"We hire the best people."

"Our people are our greatest asset."

It sounds noble. Inspirational. Very LinkedIn.

But here's the secret every high-functioning organization eventually figures out:

Great people can't save a broken system.
But a great system can save average people.

And most places have this completely backwards.

The Illusion That Talent Fixes Everything

Organizations worship talent because talent is shiny.

It gives leaders an excuse to avoid the real problem — the system.

If the system is unclear, chaotic, or drowning in contradictions, leaders blame:

- hiring
- morale
- culture
- engagement
- "communication issues"
- the alignment of Mercury in retrograde

Everything except the thing that's actually broken:

the way the work flows.

People fail not because they're incompetent,
but because the system is.

A Bad System Breaks Good People

Ask anyone who has ever worked somewhere dysfunctional:

It doesn't matter how brilliant, motivated, or ambitious you are…

If:

- everything requires ten approvals,
- priorities change hourly,
- nobody owns anything,
- decisions get reversed by committee,
- politics outrank competence,
- feedback is optional,
- and expectations are vague—

You will fail.

And then they will blame you for failing.

That's the magic trick of a bad system:
it turns competent people into exhausted ones.

The Myth of the "Hero Employee"

Every broken organization has a few "heroes."

These are the people who:
- fix everything
- answer everything
- know everything
- save everything
- and burn out quietly in a corner

Leadership praises them endlessly, saying:
"Look how committed they are!"

They never ask:

"Why do we need heroes in the first place?"

Heroes appear when the system fails.
Heroes disappear when the system works.

A functioning system doesn't need firefighters.
A failing system manufactures them.

Systems Aren't Bureaucracy — Systems Are Clarity

People hear "system" and imagine:

- red tape
- binders
- flowcharts
- corporate jargon
- HR diagrams with too many arrows

But a system is none of that.

A system is simply:

The way work actually gets done — when no one is pretending.

A good system makes things:

- predictable
- repeatable
- consistent
- clear
- less stupid

A bad system makes things:

- political
- personal
- emotional
- chaotic
- exhausting

Most organizations don't want systems.

They want heroics disguised as effort.

Why Leaders Avoid Building Systems

Systems require decisions.
Decisions require courage.
Courage requires accountability.

See the problem?

Systems force leaders to define things:
- Who owns what?
- What matters most?
- What doesn't matter at all?
- Who decides?
- What is the actual goal?
- What does "done" mean?

Most leaders don't want to define anything.

Because the moment you define something,
you can be wrong.

So instead, leaders create ambiguity—
and call it "flexibility."

It's not flexible.
It's cowardly.

Without a System, Everything Becomes Personal

When there's no system:
- people become the process
- personalities drive decisions
- emotions determine priorities
- conflicts become personal
- politics fill the gaps
- everyone has a different "right way"
- and no one agrees on anything

A system removes the guessing.

Without it, everyone builds their own universe.

And then they argue about whose universe is correct.

High Performers Love Systems

High performers look arrogant in bad systems because they refuse to drown in the nonsense.

But in good systems, they thrive.

Why?

Because systems give them:
- direction
- autonomy
- speed

- consistency
- freedom from stupidity

They don't want a "framework."
They want the ability to do their job without wrestling with dysfunction.

A system is not a cage.
A system is a runway.

Average Performers Love Good Systems Too

A shocking truth:

Most "average performers" are only average because the system is terrible.

Give them:
- clarity
- structure
- ownership
- feedback
- expectations
- fewer meetings

...and suddenly they look much more capable.

Because competence is not solely about the person.
It's about the environment they operate in.

A bad system makes people worse.
A good system makes people better.

You Don't Rise to Your Goals — You Fall to Your Systems

People love goals.
They print them on posters.
They announce them in meetings.
They recite them during performance reviews.

But goals don't change outcomes.

Systems do.

If your system is built for chaos,
your results will be chaos.

If your system is built for clear outcomes,
your results will be clear outcomes.

This is the uncomfortable truth:

People don't fail because they're lazy.
They fail because the system sets them up to fail.

The Hard Truth

People are unreliable.
People are emotional.
People are inconsistent.
People fluctuate.

Systems don't.

Systems:

- don't wake up tired
- don't forget
- don't get offended
- don't blame
- don't play politics
- don't get overwhelmed

Systems outlast talent,
outperform charisma,
and outlive ego.

People come and go.
Systems endure.

And the organizations that understand this
are the ones that win — consistently, repeatedly, predictably.

Not because they hired superheroes.
But because they built something hero-proof.

Chapter 27
Why Leadership Isn't What People Think It Is

Leadership might be the most misunderstood word in the modern workplace.

Everyone wants to be a leader, everyone claims to be a leader, and everyone is terrified you'll ask them to actually *lead* something.

Leadership has become a personality aesthetic — like wearing glasses you don't need or posting pictures of yourself reading books you never opened. It's branding, not behavior.

Most people want the appearance of leadership without the burden of leadership.

They want the spotlight, not the responsibility.

They want the praise, not the pressure.

They want the authority, not the accountability.

They want to "inspire," but not decide.

Leadership today is basically cosplay.

D.M. Christensen

The Leader People Want to Be vs. The Leader the World Actually Needs

The leader people imagine themselves as:
- charismatic
- visionary
- admired
- adored
- motivational
- brilliant
- followed by crowds
- quoted on social media in block text over a mountain sunset

The leader the world actually needs:
- decisive
- clear
- boring
- consistent
- responsible
- emotionally mature
- predictable
- willing to do the things no one else will

Guess which one people choose?

Why People Avoid Real Leadership

Real leadership is frightening because real leadership exposes you.

Once you are the one who decides:

- there is no one left to blame
- your mistakes aren't private
- your judgment is on display
- your competence is measurable
- your insecurities can't be hidden
- your excuses disappear
- and everyone sees exactly how good (or bad) you are

Most people aren't afraid of responsibility itself.
They're afraid of being seen **failing** in responsibility.

So they hide behind titles, committees, meetings, and inspirational nonsense that sounds like leadership but requires none of the courage.

The Corporate Version of Leadership Is a Joke

Corporations have turned leadership into a buffet of meaningless rituals:

- personality color quizzes
- "leadership journeys"
- inspirational posters
- trust falls
- corporate retreats with icebreakers
- self-evaluations where everyone magically becomes "above average"
- managers reading leadership books they won't apply
- leaders giving speeches about accountability they don't model

It's theater.
It's cosplay.
It's performance art for insecure adults.

Meanwhile, the actual work of leadership is rotting in the corner.

Leadership Isn't Inspiration — It's Ownership

The true definition of leadership is painfully simple:

Leadership is being the person who takes responsibility for the outcome.

Not for the credit.
Not for the applause.
Not for the narrative.
For the **outcome**.

That means you:
- decide
- clarify
- communicate
- correct
- adjust
- confront
- protect
- evaluate
- and carry the weight

Real leadership is invisible when it works and unmistakable when it doesn't.

Why Most "Leaders" Aren't Leading at All

Most leaders don't lead; they supervise.

They:
- track tasks
- attend meetings
- escalate decisions
- forward emails
- report status
- recite policies
- monitor dashboards
- avoid conflict
- pretend to give feedback
- say "we need better communication"
- and call it leadership

Supervision isn't leadership.
Administration isn't leadership.
Oversight isn't leadership.

Leadership begins where supervision ends:
when someone takes responsibility instead of waiting for someone else to.

The Ugly Secret: Leadership Isn't Glamorous

Real leadership doesn't feel like authority.
It feels like:
- stress
- pressure
- doubt
- responsibility

- weight
- making the hard call
- being the bad guy
- disappointing someone
- protecting your team
- standing alone
- and telling the truth even when it's inconvenient

Leadership isn't glamorous.
It's heavy.

That's why so many people avoid it —
they want the crown, not the weight.

High Performers Lead Without Being Asked

High performers don't wait for a title.
They don't need permission.
They don't need a badge or a certificate or a job description that says "leader."

They just step forward.

Because to them, leadership isn't ego.
It's instinct.

When something needs to be done,
they do it.

When a decision needs to be made,
they make it.

When someone needs to be protected,
they protect them.

And when something goes wrong,
they say the words most people never will:

"That's on me."

That sentence is real leadership.
Everything else is marketing.

The Hard Truth

Leadership is not about charisma, confidence, or being adored.

Leadership is not the quote you post on LinkedIn after reading two chapters of a book you abandoned.

Leadership is not a personality type.

Leadership is not a certification, a conference, or a speech.

Leadership is the willingness to be the one who carries the weight.

Most people want leadership until they feel how heavy it actually is.

The ones who don't run from it —
the ones who step forward anyway —
those are the real leaders.

Everyone else is just playing dress-up.

Chapter 28
Why People Don't Finish Things

Starting something is easy.

Finishing something is a completely different species of difficulty.

Anyone can start.

Starters are everywhere.

People start:

- diets
- projects
- hobbies
- routines
- businesses
- books
- courses
- habits
- reorganizing the garage
- "30-day challenges" they abandon by day four

But finishing?

Finishing requires a level of psychological violence most people won't commit.

The world is full of half-written novels, half-cleaned closets, half-executed ideas, and half-lived lives.

Not because people lack ambition —
but because ambition is cheap and completion is expensive.

The Beginning Is Fun. The Middle Is War.

The beginning gives you dopamine.
The middle takes it away.

The beginning feels inspiring.
The middle feels like work.

The beginning is dreams and possibility.
The middle is repetition, boredom, and self-doubt.

This is why most people never finish anything:
they confuse excitement for commitment.

When excitement fades — as it always does — they assume something is wrong.

Nothing is wrong.
They've just reached the part where emotional grit replaces enthusiasm.

Most people bow out there.

Finishing Requires Confronting Yourself

The reason people don't finish has nothing to do with time, resources, or talent.

People fail to finish because finishing forces them to confront uncomfortable questions:

- "What if this isn't as good as I hoped?"
- "What if I finish and it's not impressive?"
- "What if people judge me?"
- "What if someone actually sees my work?"
- "What if I prove I'm not as talented as I thought?"
- "What if I never get another burst of motivation?"

So they stall.
They linger.
They tweak endlessly.
They "get busy."
They promise to revisit it "soon."

Finishing forces you to face reality.
Quitting lets you keep the fantasy.

People usually choose the fantasy.

Perfectionism Is Just Fear with Better Branding

People say they don't finish because they're perfectionists.

No they aren't.
They're scared.

Perfectionism is fear wearing a suit.

It sounds noble:
- "I just want it to be great."
- "I have high standards."
- "I'm very detail-oriented."

But what they mean is:
- "I'm afraid of being judged."
- "I'm afraid of being average."
- "I'm afraid this won't live up to the version in my head."

Perfectionism isn't a standard.
It's a shield.

And finishing requires putting the shield down.

The Fear of Finality

Once you finish something, it becomes real.

A finished project can be:
- evaluated
- judged
- compared
- misunderstood
- disliked

As long as it's "in progress," it's safe.

It's pure potential, untouched by criticism.

People love potential because potential can't disappoint them.

Finishing closes the door on the imaginary perfect version.
It forces the imagined world to meet the real one.

And the real one is never as flawless as the fantasy.

Quitting Feels Like Relief — Until It Doesn't

When someone quits — or drifts away from finishing — there's an initial sense of relief.

A weight gets lifted.
The pressure disappears.
The expectations evaporate.

But then something worse arrives:
the quiet realization that they've abandoned themselves again.

Unused potential leaves a residue.
It sticks to you.

It becomes:

- regret
- resentment
- insecurity
- self-doubt
- imposter syndrome
- "Maybe I'm not cut out for this"

Every unfinished thing becomes a tiny scar.

High Performers Finish — Even When It's Awful

High performers don't finish because they love the process.

They finish because:
- completion builds identity
- results compound
- momentum matters
- action beats perfection
- finishing creates confidence
- completed work teaches more than abandoned work
- reality is better than fantasy
- discipline is more reliable than motivation

They don't wait to feel ready.

They don't wait for inspiration.

They don't wait for perfect conditions.

They finish because finishing separates amateurs from professionals.

The Secret to Finishing: Lower the Drama

Finishing isn't heroic.

It's procedural.

Most people add too much drama to the process.

They imagine finishing requires:

- inspiration
- passion
- clarity
- the right mood
- perfect timing
- a burst of motivation
- emotional alignment
- a destiny-level calling

No.

Finishing requires showing up when you don't feel like it.

The real secret to finishing anything:

Emotion is optional. Completion is not.

The Hard Truth

People don't fail because they can't start.
People fail because they never finish.

Finishing exposes reality.
Finishing tests character.
Finishing requires discipline.
Finishing demands responsibility.
Finishing requires courage.
Finishing eliminates excuses.

Starting is imagination.
Finishing is identity.

Most people don't lack the ability to finish —
they lack the willingness to face what finishing reveals.

But the people who finish —
the ones who push through boredom, fear, and self-doubt —
they build momentum, confidence, and a life that doesn't just begin things...

...but actually leads somewhere.

Chapter 29
Why People Don't Change

If human beings were good at change, gyms wouldn't sell annual memberships in January and regain custody of everyone's abandoned hopes by February.

People don't change easily.
Not because they don't want to — they absolutely do.
They fantasize about change constantly.

People dream about:
- the new version of themselves
- the healthier version
- the more disciplined version
- the more successful version
- the more confident version
- the "I finally have my life together" version

But between the fantasy and the reality sits a psychological brick wall called **effort**.

And that's where dreams go to die.

People Love the Idea of Change — Not the Cost of It

The idea of change feels amazing.

It gives people:
- dopamine
- optimism
- a story to tell
- an identity upgrade
- the chance to imagine a future where they're someone impressive

But actual change requires:
- consistency
- discomfort
- embarrassment
- discipline
- failure
- repetition
- boredom
- responsibility

People love transformations.
They're just allergic to the parts that transform them.

Why People Stay the Same (The Real Reasons)

It's not laziness.
It's not lack of intelligence.

It's not lack of opportunity.

People don't change because change threatens three things they protect at all costs:

1. Comfort

Nothing is more seductive than staying exactly where you are.

Comfort is emotional anesthesia.
It numbs the urge to improve.

2. Identity

Change requires admitting that the current version of you isn't good enough.

Most people would rather keep the flaws they know
than risk becoming a beginner again.

3. Predictability

Even a mediocre life feels safe if it's familiar.

Uncertainty terrifies people more than stagnation.

The Brain Is Designed to Resist Change

Your brain saves energy by automating everything.
It builds habits, routines, and predictable patterns because survival favors efficiency over improvement.

Your brain doesn't care if you're:
- unfulfilled
- underachieving
- wasting potential
- avoiding responsibility
- living the same year on repeat

It only cares that you're alive.

Change costs energy.
So your brain resists it — aggressively.

This is why change feels "hard."
You're fighting biology, not discipline.

Change Requires Letting Go of Who You Were

Most people can't change because they can't let go of the identity they've spent years protecting.

To change, you have to admit:
- "I was wrong."
- "I should've done better."
- "I'm not who I pretend to be."
- "I need help."
- "I built my life around habits that no longer work."

That level of honesty threatens everything people use to feel safe.

So instead of changing, they reorganize their excuses:
- "It's not the right time."
- "I'm waiting for things to calm down."
- "I just need to get motivated."
- "I'll start after vacation."
- "Next month will be better."

It won't.

People Change Only When Staying the Same Becomes More Painful

This is the uncomfortable truth most people spend their entire lives avoiding:

People don't change when they want to change.
People change when not changing becomes unbearable.

Breakthroughs happen when:
- the discomfort of stagnation outweighs the comfort of familiarity
- the consequences catch up
- the pain becomes too obvious to ignore
- the fantasy runs out of room
- the cost of avoidance becomes real

Pain moves people.
Comfort tranquilizes them.

Small Changes Feel Insignificant — So People Quit

People expect change to feel dramatic.

It almost never does.

Real change feels like:
- doing something uncomfortable
- repeatedly
- without applause
- without immediate results
- while doubting yourself
- while wanting to stop
- while no one notices
- for longer than seems reasonable

The problem is not that people can't change.
The problem is that people get bored long before change happens.

Attention spans fail faster than habits form.

High Performers Understand the Boring Part

High performers don't wait to feel inspired.

They:
- act without motivation
- repeat without reward
- commit without certainty

- adjust without ego
- continue without excitement

They understand that change is not a moment — it's a grind.

And grinding is something most people avoid with Olympic-level skill.

The Hard Truth

People don't change because change requires a level of honesty, discomfort, consistency, and responsibility they spend their entire lives avoiding.

Change means:

- you stop lying to yourself
- you stop defending your limitations
- you stop protecting your ego
- you stop excusing your habits
- you stop outsourcing responsibility
- you stop pretending the future will save you

Change is possible.
It's just emotionally expensive.

And most people would rather stay the same
than pay the price of becoming someone better.

The ones who do change —
the ones who confront the truth, embrace discomfort, and commit anyway —
build lives that look intentional, not accidental.

Everyone else stays exactly where they've always been.

Chapter 30
Why None of This Works Unless You Do

After thirty chapters of calling out human nonsense, organizational dysfunction, ego problems, comfort addictions, and the comedy of everyone trying to look competent without actually being competent, we arrive at the final truth:

None of this matters if you don't do anything with it.

Awareness without action is just entertainment.
Insight without effort is just trivia.
Understanding yourself means nothing if you don't change anything.

And this is where most people fail:
They love learning about improvement more than they love improving.

People will read entire books about growth while actively avoiding the parts of their life that require it.

They want transformation.
They just don't want to be the transformer.

People Love Information Because Information Feels Like Progress

Reading about goals feels productive.
Talking about growth feels productive.
Highlighting paragraphs feels productive.
Listening to podcasts feels productive.

But none of it is progress.

It's the simulation of progress.

If learning alone changed people, everyone with an internet connection would be unstoppable.

Instead, we are drowning in information
and starving for action.

The World Isn't Changed by Ideas — It's Changed by Implementation

Everyone has ideas.
Everyone has insights.
Everyone has potential.

Potential is worthless until you turn it into something real.

People think their lives will change when they discover:
- the right motivation
- the right book

- the right mentor
- the right strategy
- the right time
- the right mood

But lives change when people take responsibility.

Responsibility is the engine.
Everything else is decoration.

Growth Isn't About Knowing What to Do — It's About Doing What You Already Know

Most people don't need more information.
They need more courage.

They already know:
- which habits are ruining them
- which relationships are draining them
- which excuses they've polished to a shine
- which opportunities they've avoided
- which truths they've ignored
- which goals they've pretended to "not be ready for"

The issue isn't ignorance.
It's avoidance.

You don't need clarity to act.
You need honesty.

Action Forces Identity to Catch Up

People wait to feel like the kind of person who takes action.

That's backwards.

You don't wait to become confident before acting.
You act until confidence becomes the natural byproduct.

You don't wait to become disciplined before starting.
You start until discipline becomes your default.

Identity follows behavior, not the other way around.

This is why so many people stay stuck:
they wait to *feel ready* for a future that requires them to *behave differently now.*

Readiness isn't a feeling.
It's a decision.

Your Comfort Will Kill More Dreams Than Failure Ever Will

Failure scares people.
Comfort should terrify them.

Comfort:
- erodes ambition
- dissolves discipline
- numbs awareness

- buries potential
- disguises stagnation as stability
- convinces people that tomorrow will be easier than today

Failure hurts once.
Comfort hurts forever.

You don't rise to your ambition.
You fall to your habits.

And habits are built by what you choose to do when no one is watching.

The Only Thing That Actually Changes Your Life Is Behavior

Not intention.
Not potential.
Not desire.
Not passion.
Not positivity.
Not mindset.

Behavior.

What you repeatedly do shapes:
- your identity
- your results
- your opportunities
- your reputation
- your trajectory

People think their lives are shaped by big moments.
They aren't.
They're shaped by the small decisions people make every day — the decisions no one applauds.

The world rewards consistency, not occasional enthusiasm.

Nothing Works Until You Do

You can read books, take courses, hire coaches, attend seminars, and collect wisdom like Pokémon.

But nothing will change until you:

- do the uncomfortable thing
- break the old pattern
- stop lying to yourself
- start before you feel ready
- finish what you start
- confront the truth
- accept responsibility
- choose discipline over convenience
- escape the gravitational pull of your comfort zone

Growth is not an intellectual exercise.
It's a behavioral one.

The gap between who you are and who you want to be is not knowledge — it's execution.

The Hard Truth

This book won't change your life.
No book will.

Only you can do that.

Most people won't.
They'll nod along, agree with everything, feel inspired, and then go back to doing the exact same things they've always done.

But a few will act.
A few will see their patterns clearly.
A few will confront themselves honestly.
A few will choose discomfort over ease.
A few will take responsibility instead of seeking excuses.

Those people will change.
Those people will grow.
Those people will rewrite their lives with the same energy they rewrote their habits.

The rest will stay the same —
and wonder why nothing feels different.

The difference is simple:

Nothing changes unless you do.

And become a Leader of your own life.